BARCELONA AND MADRID

Travel guide 2023

Edwin Rodriguez

TABLE OF CONTENTS

INTRODUCTION

Spain, a dynamic and varied nation situated in the heart of Europe's Iberian Peninsula, draws tourists with its rich history, magnificent scenery, and engaging culture. Renowned for its balmy Mediterranean environment, Spain provides an assortment of activities that suit any traveler's interests, whether exploring ancient ruins, indulging in excellent food, or basking in the explosive rhythms of flamenco.

As the fourth-largest nation in Europe, Spain features a complex patchwork of regions, each with its own particular character and charm. From the sunny beaches of the Costa del Sol to the snow-capped peaks of the Sierra Nevada, from the busy capitals of Barcelona and Madrid to the small towns of Andalusia, Spain's geographical variety provides an abundance of chances for discovery and adventure.

Steeped in history, Spain's past is evident in its architectural wonders, including awe-inspiring churches, stately palaces, and well-preserved ancient ruins. The country's history spans millennia, from the medieval Alhambra in Granada to the Roman aqueduct of Segovia, illustrating the layers of civilizations that have molded Spain's cultural environment.

One cannot describe Spain without appreciating its vivid and passionate culture. With its soul-stirring music and dance, flamenco represents the passion and emotion that rushes through Spanish veins. From boisterous fiestas and colorful street festivals to bullfighting and the eternal custom of tapas, Spain's cultural tapestry is a feast for the senses.

Furthermore, Spain's gastronomic scene is an excellent treat for food aficionados. Indulge in enticing paella in Valencia, relish freshly caught seafood on the coastlines, and immerse yourself in tapas, where tiny plates of exquisite nibbles are designed to be shared and savored over a bottle of regional wine.

Whether you're drawn to the bustling streets of Barcelona, with its avant-garde architecture and vibrant nightlife, or the regal elegance of Madrid, a city that effortlessly blends old-world charm with modern sophistication, Spain offers a wealth of experiences that will leave you captivated and longing for more.

This travel guide will dig into two of Spain's most recognizable cities—Barcelona and Madrid. Join us as we explore the gorgeous streets, dig into the history and culture, and unearth the hidden jewels that make these cities genuinely unique places. Prepare to go on an incredible adventure across Spain's colorful tapestry and make memories that will last a lifetime.

Importance and Appeal of Barcelona and Madrid As Top Spanish Cities

As two of Spain's most important cities, Barcelona and Madrid possess tremendous significance and provide a distinct allure to tourists. Each city has particular traits and attractions, making them must-visit places for tourists experiencing Spain.

1. Barcelona: Barcelona, the cosmopolitan city of Catalonia, is famed for its avant-garde architecture, dynamic culture, and magnificent seaside environment. Here are some significant factors that add to its prominence and appeal:

- Architectural Marvels: Barcelona is identified with the architectural wonders of Antoni Gaudí, including the awe-inspiring Sagrada Familia, the whimsical Park Güell, and the astonishing Casa Batlló. The city's skyline is peppered with these amazing buildings, merging modernist features with distinctive originality.

- Cultural Richness: Barcelona's culture is a compelling combination of Catalan traditions and foreign influences. The city has various museums, art galleries, and cultural organizations, including the Picasso Museum and the Contemporary Art Museum of Barcelona (MACBA). Its thriving arts scene, colorful festivals, and energetic street acts add to a rich cultural tapestry.

- Beautiful Beaches: Barcelona boasts a good position along the Mediterranean coast, allowing tourists to sunbathe on beautiful sandy beaches. The famed Barceloneta Beach, with its busy promenade and waterfront eateries, is a favorite place for residents and visitors alike.

- Gastronomic Delights: Barcelona is a gastronomic wonderland featuring a dynamic food scene that mixes traditional Catalan cuisine with a modern flair. From tapas bars and lively food markets to Michelin-starred restaurants, Barcelona provides a broad choice of gourmet experiences to excite the taste senses.

2. Madrid: As Spain's capital and biggest city, Madrid has its own attraction and importance that make it a popular destination for tourists. Here's why Madrid stands out:

- Cultural center: Madrid is a thriving cultural center, hosting some of the world's most recognized art collections. The Prado Museum, home to paintings by Spanish artists including Velázquez and Goya, is a tribute to the city's cultural past. Other prominent museums are the Reina Sofia Museum and the Thyssen-Bornemisza Museum, presenting a complete trip through art history.

- Majestic Architecture: Madrid's architecture mixes old-world elegance with contemporary urbanization. The grandeur of the Royal Palace of Madrid, the beautiful Plaza Mayor, and the renowned Puerta del Sol reflect the city's architectural glory. Madrid's various plazas, parks, and boulevards contribute to its attraction as a gorgeous city.

- Gastronomy and Nightlife: Madrid's food scene is rich and lively, providing a huge choice of classic and creative delicacies. Madrid caters to every appetite, from tapas bars to medieval taverns to Michelin-starred restaurants. The city comes alive at night with its dynamic nightlife, where numerous pubs, clubs, and flamenco performances promise amazing nights.

- center position: Madrid's center position within Spain gives it a good base for visiting other parts of the nation. Day trips to ancient sites like Toledo and Segovia, or excursions to the wine areas of Ribera del Duero and La Rioja, are readily accessible from the capital.

Both Barcelona and Madrid feature distinct traits, delivering a combination of history, art, culture, and food that exhibit the rich beauty of Spain. Whether you want architectural marvels, cultural immersion, gastronomic pleasures, or just the magic of Spanish city life, these destinations provide a memorable vacation experience.

Overview of the book's contents and purpose

This travel handbook is aimed to give an in-depth analysis of two of Spain's most recognizable cities: Barcelona and Madrid. It strives to provide readers a thorough and practical resource for organizing their trip, finding the attractions of each city, and immersing themselves in the distinct culture and experiences these places offer.

The book is structured into numerous parts, each focused on distinct elements of travel in Barcelona and Madrid:

1. Planning Your Trip: - This chapter contains crucial information to assist readers in planning their travel, including the ideal time to visit, suggested length of stay, transit alternatives, lodging ideas, and budgeting guidelines.

2. Barcelona: - This section is devoted to Barcelona, diving into its rich history, culture, and districts. It emphasizes famous sites, like the Sagrada Familia, Park Güell, and the Gothic Quarter, as well as lesser-known jewels and unique experiences. It also offers practical information about local traditions, safety, and day trip tips.

3. Madrid: - Similarly, this part concentrates on Madrid, giving insights into its history, districts, and local traditions. It covers the city's biggest

attractions, like the Prado Museum, the Royal Palace of Madrid, and Retiro Park, while unearthing hidden gems and tips for enjoying the dynamic nightlife. It includes practical information on safety, day outings, and local manners.

4. Experiencing Spanish Culture: - This chapter digs into the more prominent features of Spanish culture beyond Barcelona and Madrid. It examines customs, festivals, food, art, architecture, and music vital to Spain's identity. It gives advice for immersing oneself in various cultural activities around the nation.

5. Practical Information: - The last chapter contains practical information for visitors, such as helpful Spanish words, money problems, communication and internet access, health and safety suggestions, and local traditions and etiquette.

The objective of this book is to serve as a complete and accurate reference, providing readers essential insights and advice to make the most of their stay in Barcelona and Madrid. It strives to enrich their travel experience by giving the historical and cultural background, emphasizing must-see sights, proposing off-the-beaten-path discoveries, and delivering practical tips to efficiently explore these places.

By combining informative descriptions, practical tips, and personalized recommendations, this guidebook seeks to empower travelers to create unique and memorable journeys through the captivating cities of Barcelona and Madrid, immersing themselves in Spain's beauty, culture, and spirit.

Chapter one

Planning Your Trip

Understanding the Best Time to Visit Barcelona and Madrid

When planning a trip to Barcelona and Madrid, it's crucial to consider the optimum time to visit to make the most of your travel experience. The temperature, festivals, and tourist seasons are vital in deciding the perfect time to visit these vibrant Spanish towns.

1. Weather and Climate: Barcelona: - Spring (April to June): Mild weather, blossoming flowers, and fewer people make it an excellent time to visit.

Average temperatures vary from 15°C to 25°C (59°F to 77°F).

- Summer (July to August): Barcelona has heavy visitor traffic throughout summer, with temperatures ranging from 20°C to 30°C (68°F to 86°F). It's the peak season, with long sunny days and bustling beach culture.

- Fall (September to October): Moderate temperatures and fewer visitors make it an excellent time to visit. Average temperatures vary from 15°C to 25°C (59°F to 77°F).

- Winter (November to March): Barcelona experiences warm winters, with temperatures ranging from 8°C to 15°C (46°F to 59°F). While less busy, certain attractions may have shortened hours during this period.

Madrid: - Spring and Fall: Madrid has a continental climate with hot summers and freezing winters. Spring (April to June) and autumn (September to

October) bring moderate temperatures ranging from 10°C to 25°C (50°F to 77°F), making it perfect for touring.

- Summer (July to August): Madrid has blistering temperatures, frequently topping 30°C (86°F). However, summer also offers bustling festivals and cultural activities.

- Winter (November to March): Winters in Madrid may be chilly, with temperatures ranging from 2°C to 12°C (36°F to 54°F). It's a calmer season with fewer visitors, and certain attractions may have reduced operating hours.

2. Festivals & Events: Barcelona:
- La Mercè celebration (September): Barcelona's most incredible street celebration, involving parades, music, and fireworks.

- Sant Jordi (April 23rd): Celebrated as the "Day of Books and Roses," the city comes alive with book fairs and exchanging roses and books.

- Primavera Sound event (Late May/Early June): A famous music event drawing worldwide performers and music aficionados.

Madrid: - San Isidro Festival (May): Madrid's biggest and most traditional festival, commemorating the city's patron saint with bullfights, concerts, and cultural activities.

- Three Kings Parade (January 5th): Colorful parade marking the entrance of the Three Wise Men, followed by floats and delivering sweets to youngsters.

- Feria de Madrid (Year-round): A lively trade fair and exposition facility holding numerous events, trade exhibitions, and conferences throughout the year.

3. Tourist Seasons: Barcelona and Madrid have peak tourist seasons throughout summer (June to August) when the cities are busy with tourists. It's crucial to realize that famous sites

may have lengthy lineups, and hotels and flights are more costly during this period. Spring and autumn combine excellent weather and fewer people, making times great for visiting the cities comfortably.

Considering criteria such as weather preferences, crowd levels, and festival interests, picking the ideal time to visit Barcelona and Madrid is subjective. Whether you like the colorful summer environment or a quiet experience during the shoulder seasons, recognizing these seasonal variations can help you plan an incredible vacation with these Spanish beauties.

Duration of Stay Recommendations

The length of your time in Barcelona and Madrid mainly relies on your particular tastes, hobbies, and the experiences you intend to have in each city. However, here are some basic guidelines to help you organize your visit:

Barcelona: - Short Stay (2-3 days): With a short stay, you may discover the significant monuments of Barcelona, such as Sagrada Familia, Park Güell, and the Gothic Quarter. Enjoy the colorful environment of La Rambla, indulge in tasty tapas, and absorb the Mediterranean ambiance. This time enables you to get a taste of Barcelona's culture and attractions.

- Medium Stay (4-5 days): Besides the key attractions, a medium stay enables you to explore the numerous areas of Barcelona, such as Eixample, Gràcia, and Barceloneta. You may visit famous institutions like Picasso Museum or take a day excursion to Montserrat or Sitges, immersing yourself more in the local culture and gastronomic delicacies.

- Long Stay (6+ days): With a more

extended stay, you may completely immerse yourself in the city's amenities. Besides the renowned places, you may dig into lesser-known jewels, join local events, and explore the secret corners of Barcelona. You'll have time to explore the thriving food markets, enjoy leisurely strolls along the seaside, and experience the busy nightlife. Additionally, you may arrange day visits to neighboring places like Girona or Tarragona, providing variations to your schedule.

Madrid: - Short Stay (2-3 days): With a short stay, you may explore the must-see sights of Madrid, including the Prado Museum, Royal Palace, and Retiro Park. Explore the ancient areas like Malasaña and appreciate the busy ambiance of Gran Vía. Indulge in excellent tapas and enjoy the bright atmosphere of the Spanish city.

- Medium Stay (4-5 days): A medium stay enables you to dig deeper into Madrid's cultural and creative landscape. You may visit other museums like the

Reina Sofía Museum or Thyssen-Bornemisza Museum. Explore the picturesque streets of La Latina and Lavapiés, eat the local food, and experience the city's active nightlife. You may also organize day visits to adjacent places like Toledo or Segovia.

- Long Stay (6+ days): With a more extended stay, you can thoroughly experience the rhythm of Madrid. Explore the many areas, find hidden treasures, and revel in the city's growing food culture. Attend local events, visit local markets, and meander around lesser-known museums and art galleries. You may also enjoy a leisurely stroll in the parks, browse at trendy shops, and soak in the dynamic ambiance of Madrid.

Remember, all guidelines are flexible, and you can always change the length of your visit depending on your tastes and available time. It's vital to balance visiting the big attractions and leaving space for serendipitous discoveries, enabling you to completely immerse yourself in the distinct ambiance of Barcelona and Madrid.

Obtaining Travel Documents, Visas, and Necessary Preparations

When planning a trip to Barcelona and Madrid, it is essential to ensure you have the necessary travel documents and make the required preparations in advance. Here are the key steps to follow:

1. Check Passport Validity: Ensure your passport is valid for at least six months beyond your departure date. If it is nearing expiration, consider renewing it before your trip.

2. Determine Visa Requirements: Check the visa requirements for your nationality and the purpose of your visit. Spain is a part of the Schengen Area.

Citizens of many countries, including the United States, Canada, Australia, and most EU countries, can enter Spain as tourists for up to 90 days without a visa. However, it is crucial to verify the specific requirements based on your country of citizenship. If a visa is required, allow ample time for the application process.

3. Apply for a Visa (if needed): If you require a visa to visit Spain, visit the official website of the Spanish Embassy or Consulate in your country to obtain detailed information about the application process, required documents, and any specific regulations. Submit your visa application well in advance to avoid any last-minute complications.

4. Travel Insurance: It is highly recommended to have travel insurance that covers medical expenses, trip cancellations, and lost or stolen belongings. Review your existing insurance coverage or consider

purchasing a travel insurance policy that suits your needs.

5. Research Health and Safety Guidelines: Check the latest health and safety guidelines for travel to Spain. Ensure you have up-to-date information regarding any vaccination requirements or health precautions recommended by health authorities.

6. Currency and Money Matters: Familiarize yourself with Spain's local currency, the Euro (€). Inform your bank or credit card company about your travel plans to avoid issues accessing your funds abroad. Consider carrying a mix of cash and cards for convenience.

7. Transportation: Research transportation options within Barcelona and Madrid. Both cities have efficient public transportation systems, including metro, buses, and trains. Consider obtaining a transportation card or pass for ease of travel.

8. Accommodation: Research and book your accommodations in advance to secure the best options within your budget. Barcelona and Madrid offer various hotels, apartments, and hostels to suit multiple preferences.

9. Language and Communication: While English is spoken to some extent in tourist areas, learning a few basic phrases in Spanish can be helpful and appreciated. Consider downloading translation apps or carrying a pocket phrasebook for accessible communication.

10. Research and Plan Activities: Create an itinerary based on your interests, considering the top attractions, cultural events, local markets, and dining experiences you want to explore. Note opening hours, ticket reservation requirements, and any specific recommendations.

By carefully following these steps, you can ensure a smooth and hassle-free travel experience to Barcelona and Madrid, allowing you to focus on enjoying the vibrant culture, history, and experiences these Spanish cities offer.

Transportation Options: Flights, Trains, and Local Transport

When traveling to Barcelona and Madrid, you have various transportation options to consider for both intercity and local transport. Understanding these options will help you navigate efficiently and maximize your trip. Here are the main transportation modes to consider:

1. Flights:
  - Intercontinental Flights: If you travel overseas, you can book international flights to Barcelona-El Prat Airport (BCN) or Madrid-Barajas Airport (MAD). These airports have connections with major cities worldwide.
  - Domestic Flights: If you plan to travel

within Spain or from other Spanish cities, you can find domestic flights that connect Barcelona and Madrid. Airlines such as Iberia, Vueling, and Ryanair operate frequent flights between cities.

2. Trains:
- High-Speed Trains: Spain has an excellent high-speed rail network, and you can travel comfortably between Barcelona and Madrid on the AVE (Alta Velocidad Española) trains. The journey takes around 2.5 to 3 hours, offering a convenient and scenic option.
- Regional Trains: Apart from high-speed trains, regional train services connect smaller towns and cities in the surrounding areas. These trains can be a good option if you plan to explore nearby destinations during your visit.

3. Local Transport:
- Metro: Both Barcelona and Madrid have efficient metro systems that provide convenient transportation within the cities. The extensive metro networks cover the most significant attractions,

neighborhoods, and transportation hubs.

- Buses: Public buses are another reliable and economical option for getting around. Barcelona and Madrid have comprehensive bus networks that reach various parts of the cities, including popular tourist areas.

- Taxis: Taxis are readily available in both cities. You can hail a taxi on the street or find them at designated taxi stands. Ensure the cab has a working meter or agree on a fare before starting the journey.

- Ride-Sharing: Services like Uber and Cabify operate in Barcelona and Madrid, providing an alternative to traditional taxis. You can use their apps to book rides conveniently.

- Bicycles: Barcelona and Madrid have bike-sharing systems, allowing you to rent bicycles for short rides within the cities. These systems are ideal for exploring specific areas or leisurely riding along the waterfront or parks.

It is important to note that Barcelona and Madrid have compact city centers, making them highly walkable. Walking can be a pleasant way to explore the main attractions and vibrant streets, especially in historic quarters.

When considering transportation options, consider travel time, convenience, cost, and personal preferences. Using a combination of flights, trains, and local transport will allow you to optimize your travel experience, giving you the flexibility to explore both cities and their surroundings efficiently.

Accommodation Suggestions and Booking Tips

When planning your stay in Barcelona and Madrid, choosing suitable accommodation is essential for a comfortable and enjoyable trip. Here are some suggestions and tips to help you find appropriate accommodations and make the booking process smoother:

1. Determine Your Budget: Start by determining your budget for accommodations. Both Barcelona and Madrid offer a range of options to suit different budgets, from luxury hotels to budget-friendly hostels and vacation rentals.

2. Research Neighborhoods: Familiarize yourself with the different neighborhoods in Barcelona and Madrid to find the one that best suits your preferences. Consider factors such as proximity to attractions, safety, local atmosphere, and accessibility to public transportation.

3. Types of Accommodation:
 - Hotels: Barcelona and Madrid have many hotels, ranging from boutique accommodations to well-known international chains. Consider the star rating, amenities, and customer reviews

to choose the right hotel.

- Apartments/Vacation Rentals: Renting an apartment or vacation rental can provide a more spacious and home-like experience. Platforms such as Airbnb, Booking.com, and HomeAway offer various neighborhood options.

- Hostels: If you're on a budget or prefer a more social environment, hostels are a great option. They offer dormitory-style rooms or private rooms at affordable rates, often with communal spaces for socializing.

4. Booking Tips:

- Book in Advance: To secure your preferred accommodation, especially during the high season, it's advisable to book well in advance. This ensures a broader selection and often better rates.

- Read Reviews: Before booking, read reviews from previous guests to gain insights into the property's cleanliness, service, location, and overall experience.

- Consider Location: Choose accommodations conveniently located near public transportation or within walking distance of attractions you plan to visit. This will save you time and make exploring the cities more accessible.

- Check Amenities: If specific amenities are essential to you, such as Wi-Fi, air conditioning, breakfast, or a fitness center, verify their availability before booking.

- Flexible Booking Options: Some booking platforms offer flexible cancellation policies, which can be helpful if your travel plans change. Be sure to review the cancellation terms before confirming your reservation.

- Contact the Property: If you have any specific requests or questions, contacting the property directly to ensure they can accommodate your needs can be helpful.

5. Considerations for Safety and Security: Prioritize safety when selecting

accommodations. Look for properties with reasonable security measures and positive reviews regarding protection. It's also wise to check if the property has a safe for storing valuables.

Following these suggestions and tips, you can find suitable accommodations in Barcelona and Madrid that align with your preferences, budget, and travel plans. Booking in advance and conducting thorough research will help ensure a comfortable and enjoyable stay in these vibrant Spanish cities.

Budgeting and Cost Considerations

When planning a trip to Barcelona and Madrid, it's essential to establish a budget and consider various cost factors to ensure a financially manageable and enjoyable experience.

Here are some key points to consider when budgeting for your trip:

1. Accommodation: The accommodation cost can vary depending on the type of lodging, location, and travel season. Determine your budget and explore different options, such as hotels, apartments, or hostels. Consider factors like proximity to attractions, amenities, and reviews to find accommodations that fit your budget and preferences.

2. Transportation: Account for transportation costs, including flights, train tickets, and local transport. Research and compare flight prices and consider booking in advance to secure better deals. Public transportation options like metros and buses within the cities are usually more affordable than taxis or ride-sharing services.

3. Meals and Dining: Barcelona and Madrid offer various options for different budgets. You can find

inexpensive tapas bars, local markets, and affordable restaurants for budget-friendly meals. If you prefer fine dining experiences, be prepared for higher costs. Consider including a mix of both affordable and splurge-worthy dining experiences in your itinerary.

4. Attractions and Activities: Research the entrance fees for popular attractions, museums, and guided tours in advance. Some attractions may offer discounted prices for students, seniors, or specific time slots. Prioritize the must-visit interests and allocate a portion of your budget accordingly.

5. Shopping and Souvenirs: Determine your shopping budget for souvenirs, local crafts, and any specific items you plan to purchase. Explore local markets, boutiques, and souvenir shops to understand the prices and allocate funds accordingly.

6. Entertainment and Nightlife: Consider any entertainment or nightlife

experiences you wish to indulge in, such as live music performances, flamenco shows, or clubbing. Research the costs associated with these activities and allocate funds accordingly.

7. Day Trips and Excursions: Barcelona and Madrid have beautiful destinations for great day trips. If you plan to explore nearby cities or attractions, consider the costs of transportation, entrance fees, and any additional expenses.

8. Miscellaneous Expenses: It's essential to factor in unforeseen or miscellaneous expenses such as travel insurance, visa fees (if applicable), currency exchange fees, and gratuities.

9. Currency Exchange and Payment Methods: Familiarize yourself with the current exchange rates and consider the best methods for currency exchange. Notify your bank or credit card company about your travel plans to avoid any issues with accessing funds or incurring high international transaction fees.

10. Contingency Fund: Setting aside a contingency fund for emergencies or unexpected expenses that may arise during your trip is advisable.

By carefully considering these budgeting tips and estimating the costs associated with accommodation, transportation, meals, attractions, and other activities, you can create a realistic budget for your trip to Barcelona and Madrid. Regularly track your expenses during your journey to ensure you stay within your planned budget and maximize your travel experience.

CHAPTER TWO

BARCELONA

Section 2.1: Welcome to Barcelona

Overview of Barcelona's History, Culture, and Significance

Barcelona, the capital of Catalonia in northeastern Spain, has a rich history, vibrant culture, and significant contributions to art, architecture, and literature. Here is an overview of Barcelona's historical and cultural background:

History
- Roman Origins: Barcelona traces its roots back to Roman times when it was known as Barcino. The Romans

established a colony here in the 1st century BC, leaving behind architectural remnants such as the Roman walls and the Temple of Augustus.

- Medieval Period: Barcelona flourished as a trading and maritime city during the Middle Ages. It became the capital of the County of Barcelona and played a prominent role in the Crown of Aragon. The influence of Gothic architecture is evident in landmarks such as the stunning Gothic Quarter and the iconic Barcelona Cathedral.

- Modernization and Catalan Identity: In the late 19th and early 20th centuries, Barcelona experienced significant growth and modernization. It became an industrial center and a hotspot for artistic and intellectual movements. The city's residents developed a strong sense of Catalan identity, which is still celebrated today.

Culture and Arts:
- Artistic Heritage: Barcelona is

renowned for its artistic heritage, particularly in modernist and Art Nouveau styles. The city's most famous exponent of modernism is architect Antoni Gaudí, whose iconic creations include the magnificent Sagrada Familia, Park Güell, and Casa Batlló. The Picasso Museum also showcases the works of the influential artist Pablo Picasso, who spent his early years in the city.

- Cultural Events: Barcelona hosts numerous cultural events, such as the Festival Grec, dedicated to performing arts, and the Mercè Festival, celebrating the city's patron saint. The city's theaters, concert halls, and music venues offer diverse performances, including opera, flamenco, and contemporary music.

- Gastronomy: Barcelona's culinary scene is a fusion of traditional Catalan cuisine and modern innovations. From the famous tapas and paella to the vibrant Boqueria Market, the city offers a gastronomic journey showcasing fresh

Mediterranean flavors.

Significance:
- Architecture and Design: Barcelona's architecture, especially the works of Antoni Gaudí, has garnered global acclaim and attracts millions of visitors each year. The city's unique blend of modernist, Gothic, and contemporary architecture creates a distinctive skyline.

- Sports: Barcelona is renowned for its passion for sports, particularly football (soccer). FC Barcelona, one of the world's most successful football clubs, calls the city home. The Camp Nou stadium is a revered pilgrimage site for football enthusiasts.

- Mediterranean Lifestyle: Barcelona's location on the Mediterranean coast contributes to its relaxed and outdoor-oriented lifestyle. The city's beautiful beaches, bustling waterfront, and warm climate make it an appealing destination for leisure and recreation.

Barcelona's history, culture, and significance make it a captivating destination for travelers seeking a mix of architectural marvels, artistic heritage, vibrant festivals, and a vibrant urban atmosphere. Exploring the city's historical landmarks, indulging in its culinary delights, and immersing oneself in its unique cultural offerings provide a truly enriching experience.

Neighborhood Highlights and Descriptions of Barcelona

Barcelona is a vibrant and diverse city with numerous neighborhoods offering unique charm and attractions. Here are some neighborhood highlights and descriptions to help you explore the different facets of Barcelona:

1. Eixample: Known for its wide, grid-like streets and iconic modernist

architecture, it is a central neighborhood showcasing Barcelona's architectural heritage. Here, you'll find the famous Passeig de Gràcia with its upscale shops, Gaudí's Casa Batlló and La Pedrera, and numerous restaurants and cafes.

2. Gothic Quarter (Barri Gòtic): Step back in time as you wander through the narrow medieval streets of the Gothic Quarter. This historic neighborhood is home to the Barcelona Cathedral, Plaça Sant Jaume, and the charming Plaça Reial. It's a hub for Gothic architecture, trendy boutiques, lively bars, and cozy cafes.

3. El Raval: El Raval is a multicultural neighborhood that has been transformed recently. It offers a mix of trendy bars, art galleries, and eclectic shops. Explore the MACBA (Museum of Contemporary Art of Barcelona) and enjoy the vibrant nightlife in this lively and dynamic part of the city.

4. Gràcia: Nestled just above the Eixample, Gràcia has a bohemian and artistic atmosphere. Its narrow streets are filled with quirky shops, local cafes, and lively squares like Plaça del Sol and Plaça de la Vila de Gràcia. The neighborhood hosts the popular Festa Major de Gràcia, a week-long street festival in August.

5. Barceloneta: Located by the sea, Barceloneta is Barcelona's old fishing district and the place to go for sun, sand, and seafood. Enjoy a stroll along the beach promenade, indulge in fresh seafood at beachside restaurants, and soak up the lively beach atmosphere. Don't miss the iconic W Barcelona hotel, shaped like a sail.

6. Poble Sec: Situated at the foot of Montjuïc, Poble Sec offers a mix of local charm and cultural attractions. Visit the beautiful gardens of Montjuïc, catch a show at the Teatre Grec, or explore the lively Carrer Blai, known for its tapas, bars, and vibrant nightlife.

7. Sant Antoni: This up-and-coming neighborhood is known for its laid-back atmosphere and the Sant Antoni Market, a food market popular among locals. The area has a growing number of trendy bars, restaurants, and boutiques, making it an excellent place for foodies and those seeking a local experience.

8. Poblenou: Once an industrial area, Poblenou has transformed into a creative and tech hub. It boasts modern architecture, wide streets, and a vibrant beachfront. Visit the innovative design hub, Disseny Hub Barcelona, and explore the trendy Rambla de Poblenou, lined with bars, restaurants, and shops.

9. Sarrià-Sant Gervasi: Situated in the upper part of Barcelona, Sarrià-Sant Gervasi is a peaceful and affluent neighborhood. It offers a quieter atmosphere, tree-lined streets, and beautiful parks. Explore the charming squares of Sarrià and indulge in the neighborhood's upscale boutiques,

gourmet restaurants, and cozy cafés.

10. El Born: Located adjacent to the Gothic Quarter and is a trendy and artistic neighborhood. Its narrow streets are filled with boutiques, art galleries, and stylish bars. Visit the striking Santa Maria del Mar church, explore the trendy shops in Carrer del Rec, and unwind in the picturesque Parc de la Ciutadella.

11. Les Corts: Les Corts is primarily a residential area known for being home to the famous FC Barcelona stadium, Camp Nou. Football enthusiasts can tour the stadium and visit the FC Barcelona Museum. The neighborhood also offers shopping opportunities at the L'Illa Diagonal shopping center and peaceful green spaces like Pedralbes Park.

12. Horta-Guinardó: Located in northern Barcelona, Horta-Guinardó is a tranquil neighborhood known for its lush greenery and scenic views. Explore the picturesque Park Güell, designed by

Gaudí, and visit the historical Horta Labyrinth Park with its beautiful gardens and maze. This neighborhood offers a more residential feel and is perfect for those seeking a peaceful retreat.

13. Sant Martí: Sant Martí is a rapidly evolving neighborhood with residential and industrial areas. It is home to the striking Torre Glòries (formerly known as Torre Agbar) and the innovative Disseny Hub Barcelona. Enjoy a leisurely stroll along the waterfront at Parc del Poblenou and visit the trendy Rambla del Poblenou with its vibrant atmosphere.

14. Sants-Montjuïc: This diverse neighborhood is home to Montjuïc Hill, a cultural and recreational hub. Explore Montjuïc Castle, the Magic Fountain of Montjuïc, and the Montjuïc Olympic Stadium. Sants-Montjuïc also houses the Fira de Barcelona exhibition center, making it a popular area for conferences and trade shows.

15. Sant Andreu: Located in the northeastern part of Barcelona, Sant Andreu has managed to maintain its small-town charm. The neighborhood features a quaint old town center, the Sant Andreu Market, and several parks where locals gather for leisure activities. Experience the relaxed atmosphere and immerse yourself in the authentic local ambiance.

Each of these Barcelona neighborhoods offers its distinct character, attractions, and atmosphere. Exploring them allows you to discover the city's culture, history, and lifestyle. Whether you're seeking historical landmarks, artistic venues, beachside vibes, or tranquil retreats, Barcelona's neighborhoods have something to offer for every visitor.

Local Customs and Etiquette in Barcelona

When visiting Barcelona, it's helpful to familiarize yourself with the local customs and etiquette to ensure a respectful and enjoyable experience. Here are some essential aspects to keep in mind:

1. Greetings: In Barcelona, greetings typically involve a handshake or a kiss on both cheeks, starting with the right cheek. However, a hug or a more casual greeting is common among friends and family. It's polite to address people using their titles (Mr., Mrs., etc.) unless invited to use their first name.

2. Punctuality: Being punctual is generally appreciated in Barcelona. Arriving on time for social or business engagements is considered respectful. However, there is often a more relaxed attitude towards punctuality in more informal settings, such as social

gatherings with friends.

3. Mealtime Customs: When dining out in Barcelona, greeting the staff upon entering a restaurant or café is customary. Spanish lunchtime is usually later than in other countries, typically served between 1:30 PM and 3:00 PM. Dinner is generally served after 8:00 PM. It's polite to wait for everyone to be performed before eating and sharing tapas or small plates is common.

4. Dress Code: Barcelona has a relatively casual dress code, especially during the daytime. However, when visiting religious sites or fine dining establishments, it's advisable to dress more formally and modestly. Beachwear is appropriate only at the beach or pool areas.

5. Language: While many locals in Barcelona speak English, it's appreciated when visitors try to learn a few basic phrases in Catalan or Spanish. Greeting locals with "Hola" (Hello) and

saying "Gràcies" (Thank you) are simple gestures that are well-received.

6. Public Behavior: Barcelona has a vibrant and lively atmosphere, but it's essential to be mindful of noise levels and respect others in public spaces. Avoid excessive noise, especially in residential areas during nighttime. It's also common to give up your seat on public transport to elderly people, pregnant women, or those with mobility challenges.

7. Tipping: Tipping in Barcelona is less common than in other countries but is appreciated for good service. A general guideline is to leave a small tip of around 5-10% of the bill if you are satisfied with the service. In upscale restaurants, a slightly higher tip may be expected.

8. Respect for Local Customs: Barcelona has a strong cultural identity, and it's essential to respect local customs and traditions. This includes

being respectful when visiting religious sites, following the rules and regulations in public spaces, and being mindful of local customs during festivals and celebrations.

9. Siesta and Late-Night Culture: In Barcelona, it is common to have a siesta, a mid-afternoon break, particularly in residential areas and smaller businesses. Many shops and businesses may close for a couple of hours during this time. It's essential to be aware of these customs and plan your activities accordingly. Additionally, Barcelona is known for its vibrant nightlife, with many restaurants, bars, and clubs open until the early morning. If you're out late, respect noise levels when returning to your accommodation.

10. Respect for Catalonian Identity: Barcelona is the capital of Catalonia, a region with a distinct identity and language. The Catalonian people take pride in their heritage and language. While many locals also speak Spanish

and English, showing an appreciation for the Catalan language and culture can be well-received. Using basic Catalan greetings like "Bon dia" (Good morning), "Bon vespre" (Good evening), or "Adéu" (Goodbye) can leave a positive impression.

11. Demonstrating Environmental Consciousness: Barcelona strongly emphasizes environmental sustainability. Recycling and using public transportation are actively encouraged. Be mindful of the city's waste management systems and make an effort to recycle properly. Use public transport, walk, or rent a bicycle to explore the city whenever possible, contributing to Barcelona's eco-friendly initiatives.

12. Beach Etiquette: Barcelona is famous for its beautiful beaches, and observing proper beach etiquette is crucial. Respect designated swimming areas and follow lifeguards' instructions for your safety. Keep the beaches clean

using designated trash bins and avoid leaving litter behind. While topless sunbathing is permitted, nude sunbathing is generally not allowed on Barcelona's public beaches.

13. Personal Space and Queuing: Like in many European cities, personal space is valued in Barcelona. Maintain an appropriate distance when interacting with others and respect their personal boundaries. When queuing, wait patiently and avoid pushing or cutting in line. Queuing etiquette is appreciated in shops, museums, attractions, and public transport.

14. Smoking Regulations: Barcelona has strict smoking regulations to protect public health. Smoking is prohibited in enclosed public spaces, including bars, restaurants, and public transportation. Be mindful of designated smoking areas and adhere to the regulations to ensure a pleasant experience for everyone.

15. Festivals and Celebrations: Barcelona is known for its vibrant yearly festivals and celebrations. If you have the opportunity to witness these cultural events, respect the traditions and customs associated with each festival. Follow any guidelines or restrictions to ensure the safety and enjoyment of all participants.

By embracing and respecting the local customs and etiquette, you can have a more immersive and enjoyable experience in Barcelona. Demonstrating cultural sensitivity and being mindful of the city's businesses allows you to connect with the locals, appreciate their way of life, and create lasting memories of your time in this captivating city.

Safety Tips and Precautions in Barcelona

Barcelona is generally a safe city, but it's always essential to take precautions to ensure a secure and enjoyable visit. Here are some safety tips to keep in mind:

1. Be Aware of Pickpockets: Barcelona has its share of pickpocketing incidents, like any major tourist destination. Keep a close eye on your belongings, especially in crowded areas such as metro stations, markets, and tourist attractions. Carry your bags in front of you and use secure closures. Avoid displaying valuable items or large sums of cash in public.

2. Use Reliable Transportation: Be cautious and monitor your belongings when using public transportation. Avoid engaging in conversations with strangers who may attempt to distract you. If taking a taxi, use licensed taxis or reputable ride-hailing services. Avoid unmarked or unofficial taxis.

3. Stay Alert at Night: While Barcelona is

generally safe at night, taking precautions is wise. Stick to well-lit and populated areas, especially if you're unfamiliar with the neighborhood. Avoid walking alone late at night, and use transportation options such as taxis or rideshares if possible.

4. Stay Informed about Current Events: Before your visit, stay informed about any current events or demonstrations in Barcelona. While peaceful demonstrations are common, it's advisable to avoid large gatherings or protests that could potentially escalate.

5. Secure Your Accommodation: Choose accommodation in safe and reputable city areas. Ensure your accommodation has proper security measures, such as secure locks and safes for your valuables. Keeping important documents and extra cash in a secure location is also a good idea.

6. Be Mindful of Scams: Like in any tourist destination, individuals may be

attempting to scam visitors. Be cautious of anyone offering unsolicited help or overly friendly gestures. Avoid street games, unofficial tour guides, and be wary of individuals who approach you with questionable intentions.

7. Respect Local Laws and Customs: Familiarize yourself with Barcelona's local laws and customs. It's crucial to adhere to the rules and regulations, including traffic laws, smoking regulations, and alcohol consumption laws. Respect the local culture and traditions to avoid any unnecessary conflicts.

8. Emergency Contact Information: Keep emergency contact numbers readily available, including the local police (112) and the embassy or consulate of your home country. It's always helpful to have these numbers accessible in case of any emergencies or incidents.

9. Stay Hydrated and Protect Yourself from the Sun: Barcelona has a

Mediterranean climate, and the summer can be hot. Stay hydrated by drinking plenty of water, especially if you're spending time outdoors. Apply sunscreen, wear a hat, and seek shade during the hottest hours of the day to avoid sunburn or heatstroke.

10. Trust Your Instincts: Finally, trust your instincts. If a situation feels unsafe or uncomfortable, remove yourself from it. Use common sense, be cautious, and be aware of your surroundings at all times.

11. Stay Connected and Share Itinerary: It's a good idea to stay connected with family or friends during your visit to Barcelona. Share your itinerary with someone you trust, including the addresses of your accommodation and any planned activities. This way, someone will know your whereabouts and assist you in an emergency.

12. Emergency Services and Medical Care: Familiarize yourself with the

location of hospitals, clinics, and pharmacies in Barcelona. Call the local emergency number (112) for immediate assistance in case of a medical emergency. It's also advisable to have travel insurance that covers medical expenses to ensure peace of mind during your trip.

13. Respect Beach Safety: Barcelona's beaches are popular attractions, but it's essential to prioritize safety while enjoying the coastal areas. Observe beach flags and signage indicating water conditions and adhere to lifeguard instructions. Be cautious of solid currents and always swim within designated spaces. Avoid leaving valuable items unattended on the beach.

14. Be Cautious with Drinks and Nightlife: When enjoying Barcelona's vibrant nightlife, it's crucial to exercise caution. Keep an eye on your drinks at all times to prevent any tampering or potential drink-spiking incidents. Stay in well-lit and populated areas, and if you

choose to drink alcohol, do so responsibly and know your limits.

15. Cultural Sensitivity: Barcelona is a diverse and multicultural city. Respecting local customs, traditions, and cultural sensitivities is important. Be mindful of appropriate attire when visiting religious sites or attending cultural events. Treat locals and fellow visitors respectfully and kindly, promoting a harmonious and inclusive environment.

16. Use Reputable Tour Operators: Choose reputable and licensed tour operators if you plan to participate in guided tours or excursions. Research reviews and recommendations beforehand to ensure your safety and the quality of the experience.

17. Secure Your Valuables: Keep your valuables secure at all times. Consider using a money belt or a secure bag to carry your passport, cash, and other vital documents. Leave unnecessary

valuables, such as expensive jewelry or excessive cash, in a secure location like a hotel safe.

18. Be Mindful of Public Wi-Fi: While Barcelona offers public Wi-Fi in many areas, exercise caution when using unsecured networks. Avoid accessing sensitive information, such as online banking, while connected to public Wi-Fi. Consider using a virtual private network (VPN) for added security.

19. Traffic Safety: When navigating Barcelona's streets, be mindful of traffic rules and pedestrian crossings. Look both ways before crossing the street, even at designated pedestrian crossings. Not all drivers may adhere to the authorities. Use pedestrian underpasses or bridges when crossing busy roads.

20. Trust Your Intuition: Ultimately, trust your intuition and instincts. If a situation or person feels unsafe or suspicious, remove yourself. Avoid isolated or poorly lit areas, especially at night. Stay

alert and aware of your surroundings to ensure your personal safety.

Incorporating these safety tips and precautions into your travel plans can enhance your security and have a worry-free experience in Barcelona. Remember that being informed, cautious, and proactive is critical to enjoying a safe and memorable trip to this vibrant city.

Section 2.2: Top Attractions in Barcelona

Sagrada Familia

Sagrada Familia, officially known as the Basilica and Expiatory Church of the Holy Family, is an iconic landmark in Barcelona, Spain. Designed by the renowned Catalan architect Antoni Gaudí, it is one of the city's most famous and visited attractions. Here's an overview of the Sagrada Familia:

1. Architectural Marvel: The Sagrada Familia is a masterpiece of architectural design and a testament to Gaudí's unique style, Catalan Modernism or Art Nouveau. Construction of the basilica began in 1882 and is still ongoing, making it an ever-evolving project. The intricate and elaborate details of the building showcase Gaudí's genius and innovative approach to architecture.

2. Religious Significance: The Sagrada Familia is a Catholic basilica dedicated to the Holy Family (Sagrada Familia in Spanish). It was envisioned as an expiatory church, a place of atonement and worship. Gaudí's design was deeply rooted in his Christian faith, and every aspect of the building reflects religious symbolism and meaning.

3. Facades: The basilica has three magnificent facades, each telling a different aspect of the life of Jesus Christ. The Nativity Façade, facing the sunrise, depicts the birth of Jesus and is adorned with intricate sculptures and scenes from the nativity. The Passion Façade, facing the sunset, portrays the crucifixion and suffering of Jesus with stark and dramatic sculptures. The Glory Façade, which is still under construction, will represent the glorification of Jesus and the final judgment.

4. Towering Spires: One of the most striking features of the Sagrada Familia is its soaring towers. When completed,

the basilica will have 18 towers, each representing different religious figures. The central tower, called the Tower of Jesus Christ, will be the tallest and stand at 172.5 meters (566 feet), making it one of the tallest religious structures in the world.

5. Interior Design: The interior of the Sagrada Familia is equally awe-inspiring. Gaudí envisioned the space to resemble a forest, with columns branching out like trees and a ceiling that resembles a canopy of leaves. The play of natural light through the stained glass windows creates a breathtaking atmosphere inside, with colors cascading across the space and filling it with a sense of spirituality and tranquility.

6. Museum and Views: The Sagrada Familia also houses a museum that provides insights into the history and construction of the basilica. Visitors can learn about Gaudí's life and see models, drawings, and exhibits showcasing the evolution of the project. Additionally,

those willing to climb the towers can enjoy panoramic views of Barcelona and appreciate the intricate architectural details up close.

7. Ongoing Construction: The construction of the Sagrada Familia has been a long and complex process, relying heavily on private donations and the dedication of countless architects, artisans, and craftsmen. While unfinished, the estimated completion date is 2026, marking the centenary of Gaudí's death.

The Sagrada Familia is an architectural gem symbol of Barcelona's rich cultural heritage, a testament to Gaudí's visionary genius. It attracts millions of visitors each year who marvel at its beauty, experiences its spiritual ambiance, and witness the ongoing creation of a true architectural masterpiece.

Park Güell

Park Güell is a unique public park located in Barcelona, Spain. Designed by the renowned Catalan architect Antoni Gaudí, it is a beautiful and whimsical space that showcases Gaudí's distinctive style and creativity. Here's an overview of Park Güell:

1. Architectural Marvel: Park Güell is a testament to Gaudí's innovative architectural vision. It was originally conceived as a housing development project commissioned by Eusebi Güell, a wealthy entrepreneur and Gaudí's patron. However, the project was unsuccessful, and the site was eventually transformed into a public park in the early 20th century.

2. Nature and Design Integration: Gaudí's design for Park Güell seamlessly blends architecture with the surrounding natural landscape. The park features winding paths, stone structures, and

colorful tile mosaics integrated harmoniously with the natural contours of the hillside. Gaudí's organic shapes, vibrant colors, and intricate detailing create a whimsical and otherworldly atmosphere.

3. Monumental Staircase and Dragon Fountain: The monumental staircase at the entrance of Park Güell is adorned with a mosaic dragon, which has become an iconic park symbol. The dragon fountain is decorated with colorful ceramic tiles, and water flows from its mouth, adding a touch of playfulness and charm.

4. Hypostyle Room: One of the highlights of Park Güell is the Hypostyle Room, also known as the Sala de les Cent Columns (Hall of the Hundred Columns). This space features a forest of stone columns that support a large terrace above. The columns, designed to resemble tree trunks, create a sense of being in a natural forest, even though they are man-made.

5. Nature Trails and Gardens: Park Güell offers several walking trails and paths that wind through lush gardens and green spaces. These trails allow visitors to enjoy nature's tranquility and discover hidden corners within the park. The carefully landscaped gardens feature a variety of Mediterranean plants, providing a serene and picturesque environment.

6. Güell's House (Casa Museu Gaudí): Located within the park, it was initially intended for Eusebi Güell. Today, it houses the Casa Museu Gaudí, a museum dedicated to Gaudí's life and works. Visitors can explore the museum and learn more about Gaudí's creative process and influence on Barcelona's architectural landscape.

7. UNESCO World Heritage Site: In recognition of its exceptional cultural and architectural significance, Park Güell, along with other works by Gaudí in Barcelona, was designated as a

UNESCO World Heritage Site in 1984. It is recognized as a masterpiece of creative genius and a reflection of Gaudí's innovative approach to architecture.

Park Güell is a captivating destination that offers a glimpse into the imagination of Antoni Gaudí. Its stunning architecture, natural beauty, and artistic details make it a must-visit attraction in Barcelona. Whether you are strolling through the gardens, marveling at the mosaic artwork, or taking in the panoramic views of the city, Park Güell promises a truly enchanting experience.

La Rambla

La Rambla, sometimes called Las Ramblas, is a busy and renowned boulevard in the center of Barcelona, Spain. It is one of the city's most famous and busiest boulevards, drawing residents and visitors alike. Here's an overview of La Rambla:

1. Pedestrian street: La Rambla is a pedestrian-friendly street extending roughly 1.2 kilometers (0.75 miles) from Plaça de Catalunya to the Columbus Monument at Port Vell. It has a spacious center pedestrian promenade bordered by small traffic lanes.

2. vibrant environment: La Rambla is recognized for its vibrant and busy environment. The street is flanked by many stores, cafés, restaurants, street entertainers, flower sellers, and news kiosks. The lively energy, continual hum of activity, and unusual mix of people create a distinct and intriguing ambiance.

3. Cultural and Historical sites: Along La Rambla, you'll discover various noteworthy places and areas of interest. These include:

- Plaça de Catalunya: Located at the

northern end of La Rambla, this central area serves as a major transit hub and a popular gathering spot.

- Boqueria Market: Situated halfway down La Rambla, the Mercat de Sant Josep de la Boqueria, generally known as Boqueria Market, is a bustling food market where you can discover an abundance of fresh produce, local specialties, and culinary pleasures.

- Gran Teatre del Liceu: This ancient opera theatre, established in 1847, is famous for its outstanding performances and gorgeous architecture. It is situated around the midway of La Rambla.

- Miró Mosaic: As you wander down La Rambla, you'll see a mosaic created by the famed Catalan artist Joan Miró. The mosaic is embedded in the pavement and is a popular site for photography and a symbol of the city's creative legacy.

- Columbus Monument: The majestic Columbus Monument sits at the southern end of La Rambla, near the Port Vell port. The monument celebrates Christopher Columbus and his contribution to finding the Americas.

4. Street entertainers: La Rambla is famed for its street entertainers, called "estatuas vivientes," or living statues. These brilliant artists dress up in extravagant costumes and masterfully pose as statues, dazzling passersby with their performances. It's a compelling sight and a chance to connect and snap photographs with these distinctive people.

5. Outdoor Cafes and Dining: Along La Rambla, various outdoor cafes and restaurants allow relaxing and taking up the ambiance while enjoying a meal or a cool drink. From traditional Catalan cuisine to foreign cuisines, there is a vast choice of eating alternatives to accommodate varied preferences.

6. Promenade and People-Watching: La Rambla is a beautiful area for a leisurely walk. The center promenade is decorated with trees, offering shade and a nice setting. It's a favorite area for residents and tourists to take a leisurely stroll, people-watch, or just rest on one of the numerous seats and absorb the colorful environment.

7. Shopping & Souvenirs: La Rambla provides a diversified shopping experience with great stores and boutiques. You may discover anything from apparel and accessories to unique souvenirs, crafts, and traditional Catalan items. It's a terrific spot to shop and find keepsakes to remember your vacation to Barcelona.

La Rambla is a hallmark of Barcelona's lively culture, busy street life, and numerous attractions. It provides a unique combination of history, entertainment, shopping, and food, making it a vital visit for anybody touring the city. However, it's vital to keep a few things in mind when visiting La Rambla:

8. Pickpocketing Awareness: La Rambla may attract pickpockets like any renowned tourist area. Be aware of your things and keep an eye on your personal stuff at all times. Avoid carrying significant quantities of cash, and try wearing a money belt or keeping your valuables protected in a bag near your body.

9. Street Vendors & Scams: While strolling down La Rambla, you may see street vendors offering different products, including souvenirs, flowers, or street art. Be aware of pushy sellers or those participating in fraud. Exercise your judgment and be aware of any strange activities or demands for money.

10. Nighttime Safety: While La Rambla is typically secure during the day, it's important to take additional care while visiting at night. Stick to well-lit places and avoid straying off onto remote side alleys. Travel in groups whenever

feasible, and if you want to remain out late, ensure you have a dependable way of transportation back to your hotel.

11. Respect Public Spaces: La Rambla is a shared public place. Therefore, respecting the environment and the people around you is crucial. Avoid littering and use designated garbage containers. Be aware of noise levels, particularly in the late hours, to provide a good experience for everyone.

12. Local Customs and Etiquette: Barcelona has distinct customs and etiquette. While wandering down La Rambla, remember to greet residents with a pleasant "Hola" and be mindful of their personal space. Follow local conventions while eating, such as waiting for a waiter to deliver the bill and saying "por favor" (please) and "gracias" (thank you) when conversing with natives.

La Rambla provides a vivid and dynamic experience, displaying the spirit of

Barcelona's street life and culture. By keeping vigilant, respecting the surroundings, and enjoying the spirit of the boulevard, you may thoroughly enjoy exploring this historic street in Barcelona.

Casa Batlló

Casa Batlló is a remarkable architectural masterpiece in the middle of Barcelona, Spain. Designed by the great Catalan architect Antoni Gaudí, it is a monument to his artistic brilliance and unique approach to architecture. Here's an overview of Casa Batlló:

1. Architectural Marvel: Casa Batlló is an exemplary example of Gaudí's distinctive style, referred to as Catalan Modernism or Art Nouveau. Built between 1904 and 1906, it is notable for its organic patterns, intricate

craftsmanship, and imaginative use of materials. The edifice stands out as a captivating blend of art and architecture.

2. Unique Façade: The exterior of Casa Batlló is a remarkable showcase of Gaudí's inventiveness. The façade is adorned with a colorful mosaic of broken ceramic tiles, known as trencadís, producing a mosaic effect that shimmers in the daylight. The undulating curves, skeletal balconies resembling masks, and the absence of straight lines are hallmarks of Gaudí's organic architectural style.

3. Symbolic Interpretation: Gaudí's design for Casa Batlló blends symbolic symbols inspired by nature and Catalan culture. The façade is supposed to represent the scales of a dragon, with the balcony pillars portraying the bones of the monster's victims. The rooftop, with its mosaic chimneys, is reminiscent of a fabled dragon's back.

4. interior Design: Casa Batlló's interior

is equally gorgeous as its façade. Gaudí created the interiors carefully, mixing flowing lines, carved woodwork, and stained glass windows to create a harmonious and immersive experience. The rooms exhibit Gaudí's unique use of light, color, and natural forms.

5. Noble level: The noble level of Casa Batlló, where the Batlló family dwelt, is a lovely space filled with excellent craftsmanship. The primary rooms, such as the living and dining rooms, display exquisite details, including finely molded ceilings and gently curved furniture. Employing vibrant colors and natural light helps create a unique ambiance.

6. Rooftop Terrace: Casa Batlló's rooftop is a notable construction aspect. It is adorned with colorful mosaic tiles and distinctive chimney stacks that resemble medieval soldiers. The rooftop affords panoramic views of Barcelona and is an excellent vantage point to see the architectural complexities of Casa Batlló and the surrounding cityscape.

7. Museum and Cultural Space: Casa Batlló presently works as a museum and cultural space, allowing visitors to study the building's history and learn about Gaudí's architectural vision. The museum chronicles the evolution of Casa Batlló. It provides insights into Gaudí's life and works with interactive displays and multimedia presentations.

Casa Batlló is an homage to Gaudí's creativity and contribution to Barcelona's architectural environment. Its beautiful façade, imaginative interior, and inclusion of symbolism make it a must-visit location for art and architecture aficionados. Exploring Casa Batlló affords a unique opportunity to appreciate Gaudí's creative genius and immerse oneself in the grandeur of his architectural masterpiece.

Gothic Quarter

The Gothic Quarter, often known as Barri Gòtic, is a historic area in the center of Barcelona, Spain. It is noted for its tiny medieval alleyways, historic buildings, and rich cultural history. Here's an overview of the Gothic Quarter:

1. Historical Significance: The Gothic Quarter is vital to Barcelona's history. It is the oldest portion of the city, going back to Roman times when it was known as Barcino. Walking through its convoluted lanes, you may view layers of history, from Roman remains to Gothic and medieval architecture.

2. Architectural Marvels: The Gothic Quarter features a magnificent collection of architecture comprising structures from diverse eras. Gothic-style architecture dominates the area, such as the Barcelona Cathedral (Catedral de Barcelona) and the Basilica of Santa Maria del Mar. The exquisite

detailing, towering spires, and ornate facades emphasize the majesty of Gothic architecture.

3. Quaint lanes and Plazas: Exploring the Gothic Quarter involves meandering through small, twisting lanes that take you back in time. The atmospheric streets are packed with attractive stores, cafés, and boutiques. Plaça del Pi and Plaça Sant Felip Neri are gorgeous squares where you can relax and enjoy the vibe.

4. Carrer del Bisbe: One of the prominent avenues in the Gothic Quarter is Carrer del Bisbe, noted for its archway linking the Palau de la Generalitat (the seat of the Catalan government) and the Casa dels Canonges. The archway is embellished with exquisite carvings and is a popular place for pictures.

5. Roman Remains: The Gothic Quarter has some well-preserved relics of the Roman period. The Barcelona City History Museum in the Gothic Quarter

gives a peek into the city's Roman history via its subterranean archaeological site. Visitors may explore the remnants of ancient Roman streets, houses, and even an old washing facility.

6. Plaça Reial: Plaça Reial is a lively plaza that serves as a dynamic center of activity in the Gothic Quarter. It is lined with palm palms and boasts lovely neoclassical buildings and a central fountain. The area is recognized for its vibrant ambiance, prominent eateries, and buzzing nightlife.

7. Cultural treasures: Besides its architectural glories, the Gothic Quarter is home to various cultural treasures. The Picasso Museum, situated in the area, features an extensive collection of works by the famous artist Pablo Picasso. The Museum of the History of Barcelona (MUHBA) gives more profound insights into the city's history and legacy.

8. Shopping and Gastronomy: The Gothic Quarter provides a comprehensive shopping experience with boutique boutiques, antique shops, and handcrafted crafts. You may get unusual souvenirs, current apparel, and traditional Catalan items. The district is especially recognized for its gastronomic scene, with various restaurants, tapas bars, and traditional diners offering Catalan delicacies.

The Gothic Quarter is a compelling district that embodies the spirit of Barcelona's rich history and architectural splendor. Its tiny alleyways, ancient structures, and bustling atmosphere make it a must-visit location for visitors wishing to immerse themselves in the city's cultural legacy. Exploring the Gothic Quarter is like entering a living museum, where the past combines with the present to produce a unique experience.

Montjuïc

Montjuïc is a famous hill situated near Barcelona, Spain. It provides a multitude of attractions, breathtaking vistas, and a rich historical and cultural importance. Here's an overview of Montjuïc:

1. Natural Setting: Montjuïc is a hill that rises roughly 173 meters (568 feet) above sea level, offering a natural vantage point viewing Barcelona and the surrounding surroundings. The hill is surrounded by rich foliage, giving a calm getaway from the hectic metropolis below.

2. Panoramic Views: From the summit of Montjuïc, tourists are rewarded with stunning panoramic views over Barcelona, the Mediterranean Sea, and the surrounding countryside. The perspective encompasses prominent locations such as Sagrada Familia, Port Vell, and the Barcelona shoreline, offering an excellent background for

extraordinary images.

3. Historical Significance: Montjuïc has played a key part in Barcelona's history. The hill was previously home to a fortification, which has seen countless historical occurrences. It functioned as a critical military site and a symbol of resistance throughout the Spanish Civil War. Today, the remnants of the stronghold may still be visited, revealing insights into the city's history.

4. Montjuïc Castle: Atop the hill sits the majestic Montjuïc Castle (Castell de Montjuïc). It was initially constructed as a military castle in the 17th century and has served many uses. Visitors may visit the castle, explore its gardens, and enjoy spectacular views of Barcelona. The castle now accommodates exhibits and cultural activities that emphasize its historical relevance.

5. Olympic Legacy: Montjuïc played a significant role during the 1992 Summer Olympics in Barcelona. The hill held

various Olympic events, including the opening and closing ceremonies. The Olympic Stadium, refurbished for the games, is situated in Montjuïc and continues hosting athletic events and concerts.

6. Parks and Gardens: Montjuïc has beautiful parks and gardens that give a tranquil getaway from the metropolitan surroundings. The Montjuïc Park, constructed neoclassically, contains beautiful green areas, fountains, and statues. The Botanical Garden shows a vast diversity of Mediterranean and worldwide plant species. At the same time, the Joan Brossa Gardens provide creative pieces and spectacular vistas.

7. Cultural Attractions: Montjuïc is home to several cultural attractions. The Magic Fountain of Montjuïc is a must-see extravaganza that mixes light, music, and water, producing a stunning performance. The Montjuïc Olympic Ring, with its distinctive telecommunications tower, sports

facilities, and the Palau Sant Jordi, is a tribute to the Olympic heritage.

8. Museums and Cultural Institutes: Montjuïc includes various museums and cultural institutes. The National Museum of Catalan Art (MNAC) shows a vast collection of Catalan artwork, including Romanesque and Gothic masterpieces. The Joan Miró Foundation showcases the works of the famous Catalan artist Joan Miró. At the same time, the Caixa Forum organizes rotating exhibitions and cultural activities.

Montjuïc is a diverse destination that blends natural beauty, historical relevance, and cultural attractions. Its commanding vistas, numerous goods, and quiet environment make it a clear spot to discover when visiting Barcelona. Whether you're interested in history, wildlife, or just enjoying magnificent views, Montjuïc provides an immersive experience showing this bustling city's beauty and attractiveness.

Barcelona Beaches

Barcelona is endowed with a spectacular coastline that spans the Mediterranean Sea, allowing tourists to enjoy lovely sandy beaches in the center of the city. The beaches of Barcelona are famed for their dynamic ambiance, crystal-clear seas, and a variety of services that appeal to both residents and visitors. Here's a deeper look at Barcelona's beaches:

1. Barceloneta Beach: Barceloneta Beach is the most renowned and famous beach in Barcelona. Located in the area of Barceloneta, it is conveniently accessible from the city center. This famous beach is noted for its beautiful beaches, bustling promenade, and many beachside cafés and restaurants. It provides numerous amenities such as sun loungers, umbrellas, showers, and lifeguard services. Barceloneta Beach is great for sunbathing, people-watching, and

beachfront sports like beach volleyball and paddleboarding.

2. Nova Icaria Beach: A short walk from Barceloneta Beach is Nova Icaria Beach. This beach is less busy and provides a more relaxing vibe. With its considerable area, smooth beaches, and tranquil waves, it is a good option for families and anyone wanting a peaceful beach experience. Nova Icaria Beach has amenities, including showers, sports facilities, and beach bars. It is a handy site for relaxation and entertainment.

3. Bogatell Beach: Situated northeast of Barceloneta Beach, Bogatell Beach is another popular beachgoer location. With its extensive shoreline and well-maintained beaches, it draws both residents and visitors alike. Bogatell Beach has a calm ambiance compared to Barceloneta, making it a perfect site for people seeking leisure. The beach is well-equipped with services such as showers, changing rooms, and sports grounds, making it ideal for numerous

beach activities.

4. Mar Bella Beach: Located to the east of Barceloneta Beach, Mar Bella Beach is recognized for its young and dynamic environment. It acquired famous as Barcelona's unofficial nudist beach, drawing a mixed audience. Mar Bella Beach provides a more liberal, open-minded culture with dedicated clothing-optional sections. It is also a center for water sports lovers, providing windsurfing, kiteboarding, and beach volleyball facilities.

5. other Beaches: Besides the main beaches described above, Barcelona offers numerous famous beaches worth investigating. These include Nova Mar Bella Beach, situated near Mar Bella Beach and recognized for its clear waters and serene setting, as well as the quieter beaches of Nova Mar Bella and Llevant.

Whether you're seeking a bustling beach experience or a calm getaway by the sea,

Barcelona's beaches provide a choice of possibilities to suit various interests. With their scenic locations, handy amenities, and the background of Barcelona's dynamic metropolis, these beaches give an ideal chance to relax, soak up the sun, and enjoy the Mediterranean charm of the city.

Section 2.3: Beyond the Mainstream

Hidden Gems and off-the-beaten-path locations

Barcelona is a city full of surprises, and beyond its main attractions, countless hidden treasures and off-the-beaten-path sites are waiting to be found. These lesser-known sites give a distinct and genuine peek into the local culture and provide a respite from the hectic tourist hordes. Here are some hidden beauties in Barcelona worth exploring:

1. El Raval: Situated just off La Rambla, El Raval is a colorful and dynamic area with a bohemian ambiance. It's a melting pot of diverse cultures and provides many art galleries, fashionable bars, and interesting boutiques. Explore its small lanes covered with street art, visit the Contemporary Art Museum of Barcelona (MACBA), or rest in the secret squares such as Plaça dels Àngels.

2. Bunkers del Carmel: For panoramic views of Barcelona, travel to Bunkers del Carmel. Located in El Carmel, these old anti-aircraft bunkers give stunning views of the city skyline. It's a local secret and a fantastic area to have a sunset picnic or snap gorgeous shots.

3. Sant Pau Recinte Modernista: Often overshadowed by Gaudí's creations, Sant Pau Recinte Modernista is a hidden treasure of modernist architecture. This

UNESCO World Heritage site was previously a hospital and boasts spectacular structures created by Lluís Domènech I Montaner. Explore the exquisite detailing and brilliant tile work of this architectural marvel.

4. Horta Labyrinth Park: Escape the urban rush and immerse yourself in the peacefulness of Horta Labyrinth Park. Located in the Horta-Guinardó area, this hidden treasure has a lovely neoclassical garden with towering hedges, statues, and a labyrinth to get lost in. It's a calm hideaway away from the city throng.

5. Gràcia neighborhood: While not entirely off the main path, the Gràcia neighborhood provides a local and genuine vibe away from the tourist-heavy districts. Stroll through its picturesque alleyways with unique stores, pleasant cafés, and bustling squares like Plaça del Sol. Visit the Festes de Gràcia in August, when the neighborhood streets are covered with

beautiful displays.

6. Montjuïc Cemetery: Montjuïc Cemetery may appear odd, but it is a fantastic site. Located on the slopes of Montjuïc Hill, this cemetery is a lovely and tranquil environment filled with magnificent tombstones and sculptures. It gives a thoughtful and introspective ambiance, revealing insights into Barcelona's history and craftsmanship.

7. Can Framis Museum: Tucked away in the Poblenou area, the Can Framis Museum is a hidden treasure for art connoisseurs. This modern art museum highlights the work of Catalan artists from the 1960s forward. The building is a refurbished factory, lending an industrial flavor to the museum. Explore its thought-provoking exhibits and discover burgeoning local talent.

8. Carrer del Bisbe: Step into the Gothic Quarter and find the magnificent Carrer del Bisbe (Bishop's Street). This tiny, ancient lane links the Barcelona

Cathedral with the Palau de la Generalitat, the seat of the Catalan government. Admire the beautiful Gothic architecture, especially the landmark bridge studded with gargoyles and the famed "Kiss of Freedom" painting.

9. Sant Antoni Market: While the Boqueria Market may be the most renowned, locals know that Sant Antoni Market is a hidden treasure for foodies. Located in the Sant Antoni area, this market provides a laid-back ambiance with a great assortment of fresh vegetables, artisanal items, and local delicacies. Take a leisurely walk around the market, eat dinner at one of the tapas restaurants, or peruse the used book market on Sundays.

10. El Born Cultural Center: Housed in a wonderfully renovated market building, the El Born Cultural Center gives a fascinating peek into Barcelona's medieval history. Located in the fashionable El Born district, this cultural center shows the archaeological

remnants of the neighborhood's old habitation, returning to the 18th century. Explore the subterranean ruins and learn about the city's history via interactive exhibitions and multimedia displays.

11. Casa Vicens: As one of Antoni Gaudí's lesser-known masterpieces, Casa Vicens is a hidden treasure for architectural fans. This early masterwork of Gaudí, situated in the Gràcia area, exhibits a unique combination of Moorish, Oriental, and Catalan architectural traditions. Explore the bright ceramic tiles, elaborate features, and lush gardens that make this mansion a hidden gem.

12. Poble-sec: While the area of Poble-sec is somewhat off the beaten path, it provides a more local and genuine experience than the city center. Located at the foot of Montjuïc hill, Poble-sec is recognized for its vibrant ambiance, traditional taverns offering vermouth, and superb range of local eateries. Explore Carrer Blai, a busy street with

tapas restaurants, and experience the neighborhood's thriving nighttime scene.

By traveling off the well-trodden road and uncovering these hidden jewels, tourists may unearth the lesser-known wonders Barcelona offers. These distinctive venues give a chance to engage with the local culture, architecture, art, and gastronomic pleasures that make Barcelona a city full of surprises.

Quirky museums and art galleries

Barcelona is recognized for its dynamic arts scene, and beyond the standard museums and galleries, the city is also home to some unique and unorthodox museums and art venues. These unusual places provide a distinct and sometimes surprising viewpoint on art, history, and society. Here are some offbeat museums and art galleries in Barcelona worth exploring:

1. Museum of Illusions: Step into a realm of optical illusions and mind-bending displays at the Museum of Illusions. Located in the center of Barcelona, this interactive museum enables visitors to explore diverse installations and participate in visual illusions that test vision. From gravity-defying chambers to holograms and mirror mazes, this museum ensures a thrilling and mind-expanding experience.

2. Museu de la Xocolata (Chocolate Museum): Chocolate enthusiasts will rejoice at the Museu de la Xocolata, a museum entirely devoted to the history and craftsmanship of chocolate. Located in the Born area, this museum features chocolate sculptures, exhibits on the origins of cocoa, and even provides workshops where visitors may manufacture their chocolate delicacies. Remember to visit the chocolate store for beautiful keepsakes.

3. El Bosc de les Fades (woodland of the Fairies): Step into a fantastical world at El Bosc de les Fades, a unique bar and art installation that recreates an enchanting woodland. Located off La Rambla, this eccentric place has fairy lights, gushing waterfalls, and realistic sculptures of fairies and magical animals. Enjoy a drink or snack while immersing yourself in this enchanting setting.

4. Hash Marihuana & Hemp Museum: For those interested in the history and cultural importance of cannabis, the Hash Marihuana & Hemp Museum provides an enlightening and thought-provoking experience. Located in the Gothic Quarter, this museum highlights the plant's numerous uses throughout history, medicinal purposes, and cultural significance. Discover ancient relics, interactive exhibitions, and informative presentations on this challenging issue.

5. Museu de Carrosses Fúnebres

(Funeral Carriages Museum):

Delve into the exciting world of funeral processions and carriages at the Museu de Carrosses Fúnebres. Housed inside the Poble-sec Cemetery, this museum shows a collection of elegant funeral carriages from various historical periods. Gain insights into funeral rituals, traditions, and the artistry behind these ornate vehicles.

6. CaixaForum: While not precisely quirky, CaixaForum gets a mention for its distinctive architectural style. This cultural institution near Montjuïc Hill contains a remarkable vertical garden built by famous botanist Patrick Blanc. The lush flora covering the outside of the building offers a dramatic contrast against the modernist façade, making it a remarkable combination of art, nature, and architecture.

Barcelona's offbeat museums and art galleries provide an alternate and unique way to understand art, history, and culture. By visiting these eccentric venues, tourists may indulge in unusual experiences, engage their senses, and get new views on the fascinating world of art and human ingenuity.

Unique culinary experiences and local markets

Barcelona is a city that tantalizes the taste senses with its varied gastronomic scene. Beyond the usual restaurants, the city offers unique culinary experiences and thriving local markets where tourists may immerse themselves in the tastes and ingredients of Catalan cuisine. Here are some unique gastronomic experiences and local markets in Barcelona worth exploring:

1. La Boqueria Market: La Boqueria is one of Barcelona's most renowned and bustling marketplaces. Located off La Rambla, it is a food lover's heaven. Explore the booths stocked with

beautiful fruits, fresh seafood, fragrant spices, and a range of local items. Sample tasty tapas and freshly squeezed juices, or indulge in jamón ibérico. La Boqueria is a feast for the senses, delivering an authentic experience of Barcelona's gastronomic delicacies.

2. Santa Caterina Market: Just a short walk from the Gothic Quarter, Santa Caterina Market is a hidden treasure that provides a more local and laid-back market experience. Recently refurbished, this market is recognized for its contemporary architecture and colorful, undulating ceiling. Discover a wide choice of fresh vegetables, handmade items, and traditional Catalan ingredients. Enjoy a dinner at a market's tapas bars or take some picnic provisions for a gourmet adventure.

3. Cooking Classes and Food Tours: Immerse yourself in Catalan cuisine by taking a cooking class or food tour in Barcelona. Learn to cook classic meals

like paella, Catalan-style tapas, or creamy crema catalana. Experienced chefs will take you through the process, revealing culinary secrets and local perspectives. Additionally, food excursions allow visitors to visit Barcelona's districts, sample authentic tastes from local cafes, and develop a greater appreciation of the city's gastronomic past.

4. Vermouth Experience: Vermouth retains a distinct position in Barcelona's gastronomic culture. Indulge in a vermouth experience where you can learn about the history and manufacture of this delicious fortified wine. Visit vermuterias and classic vermouth bars, and enjoy several vermouth varietals combined with local foods like olives, anchovies, and boquerones. This is a terrific opportunity to immerse oneself in a treasured local ritual.

5. Hidden Tapas Bars: Barcelona has countless hidden tapas bars, known as "bodegas" or "tavernas." These lovely

and often modest places provide a genuine and local tapas experience. Wander through the tiny lanes of districts like El Raval or El Born, and you may stumble across these hidden jewels. Enjoy a sip of vermouth or a cool caña (small beer) with delectable tapas, such as patatas bravas, croquettes, or grilled octopus.

6. Espai Sucre: Espai Sucre provides a unique dessert-eating experience for those with a sweet craving. This creative restaurant specializes in sweet delicacies and provides a multi-course tasting menu solely devoted to sweets. Discover unique taste combinations and stunning presentations, and explore the frontiers of dessert cuisine. Espai Sucre is a fascinating and unique gastronomic trip for dessert aficionados.

By visiting the local markets, partaking in cooking lessons, indulging in vermouth experiences, finding secret tapas restaurants, and savoring unique dessert eating, guests may go on a culinary adventure that shows Barcelona's lively tastes and culinary traditions. These encounters give a natural flavor of the city's gastronomy and provide a more excellent knowledge of Catalan food and culture.

Recommended day trips from Barcelona

Barcelona is a compelling city and a gateway to several exceptional day trip locations. If you have the time, traveling outside Barcelona lets you discover charming seaside villages, old ruins, and breathtaking natural scenery. Here are some suggested day excursions from Barcelona:

1. Montserrat: Located about an hour outside Barcelona, Montserrat is a magnificent mountain range noted for its serrated peaks and the Benedictine abbey of Santa Maria de Montserrat.

Take a picturesque train journey and cable car to reach the peak, where you may tour the monastery, see the Black Madonna, and enjoy panoramic views of the surrounding landscape.

2. Sitges: Situated only 35 kilometers southwest of Barcelona, it is a picturesque seaside town famed for its magnificent beaches, active nightlife, and rich cultural past. Stroll down the promenade, relax on the sandy shoreline, explore the tiny lanes dotted with colorful buildings, and visit the renowned Sitges Art Museum. Sitges also holds several cultural events annually, including the acclaimed Sitges Film Festival.

3. Girona: Approximately 100 kilometers north of Barcelona is the medieval city of Girona. This lovely city has a well-preserved Old Town with cobblestone streets, medieval city walls, and a gorgeous cathedral. Explore the Jewish Quarter, meander along the Onyar River adorned with colorful buildings, and

explore the magnificent Girona Cathedral featured in the TV series "Game of Thrones."

4. Tarragona: Tarragona, situated around 100 kilometers southwest of Barcelona, is a treasure trove of Roman remains and Mediterranean beauty. Discover the old Roman amphitheater overlooking the sea, see the archaeological site of Tarraco, a UNESCO World Heritage site, and meander through the small alleyways of the Old Town. Take advantage of the opportunity to relax on the magnificent sandy beaches that cover the coastline.

5. Costa Brava: If you're seeking spectacular seaside scenery, a day trip to the Costa Brava is a must. This rough and scenic stretch of coastline begins just north of Barcelona and stretches up to the French border. Explore picturesque beach villages like Cadaqués, noted for its white-washed buildings, and enjoy the crystal-clear waters of the Mediterranean. Visit the

Salvador Dalí House-Museum in Portlligat or the stunning clifftop castle at Tossa de Mar for an unforgettable experience.

6. Penedès Wine area: Wine connoisseurs might take a day trip to the Penedès wine area southwest of Barcelona. This region is recognized for producing Cava, a sparkling wine, and other high-quality wines. Take a guided tour of vineyards and wineries, taste various varietals, and learn about winemaking. Some trips also allow participating in grape picking or blending seminars.

These day excursions from Barcelona give a wide variety of activities, enabling you to discover historical monuments, appreciate coastline beauty, indulge in wine tasting, and immerse yourself in the area's rich cultural legacy. Whether you seek natural beauty or cultural riches, these sites are worth visiting to enrich your Barcelona experience.

Chapter Three

Madrid

Section 3.1: Welcome to Madrid

Introduction to Madrid's History, Culture, and Ambiance

Madrid, the dynamic capital of Spain, is a city steeped in ancient history, decorated with awe-inspiring architecture, and vibrating with a thriving cultural scene. From its roots as a Moorish stronghold to its prominence as a worldwide city, Madrid offers an intriguing combination of heritage and innovation. Here's an introduction to Madrid's history, culture, and ambiance:

History: Madrid's history extends back to the 9th century when it was created as a minor Muslim enclave known as

Mayrit. However, it was not until 1561, during the reign of King Philip II, that Madrid became the capital of Spain. Madrid saw tremendous alterations throughout the years, including developing large boulevards, exquisite squares, and towering structures. The city has experienced the rise and fall of empires, the turmoil of wars, and the cultural blossoming of the Spanish Golden Age.

Culture: Madrid is a cultural center that supports creative expression in all its manifestations. The city is home to world-class institutions, including the Prado Museum, which has an unparalleled collection of European art, including masterpieces by Goya, Velázquez, and El Greco. The Reina Sofia Museum highlights contemporary and modern art, including Picasso's classic Guernica. Madrid also features various theaters, opera houses, and music venues, where acts ranging from classical to flamenco and contemporary may be experienced.

The city's enthusiasm for football is unsurpassed, with Real Madrid and Atlético Madrid being two of the world's most successful and known football teams. The atmosphere during a match at the Santiago Bernabeu or Wanda Metropolitano stadiums is tremendous, showing the city's enthusiasm for the beautiful game.

Madrid's food culture is a feast for the senses, with innumerable pubs, restaurants, and old taverns dishing up a vast assortment of scrumptious meals. From tapas and cocido madrileño (a hearty chickpea stew) to churros and chocolate, Madrid provides a gourmet experience that exhibits the complexity and tastes of Spanish food.

Ambiance: Madrid radiates a dynamic and energetic ambiance that captivates tourists. The city comes alive with busy streets, bustling plazas, and an exuberant enthusiasm for life. The vibrant Puerta del Sol serves as the metaphorical heart of Madrid, where people and visitors converge to celebrate, greet the New Year, and absorb the city's ambiance. The Gran Vía, a lively road packed with theaters, stores, and famous buildings, pulsates with activity day and night. The city's parks, such as Retiro Park, offer calm oases where one may rest, have a picnic, or take a leisurely walk.

Madrid's residents, Madrileños, are recognized for their warm hospitality and passion for enjoying life's joys. Whether drinking coffee in a typical café, mingling at a busy tapas bar, or participating in the city's colorful nightlife, Madrileños appreciate savoring each moment.

In short, Madrid provides an intriguing combination of history, culture, and ambiance. Its great architecture, world-class museums, active cultural scene, gastronomic pleasures, and welcoming environment make it an attractive destination for visitors wishing to immerse themselves in the heart and spirit of Spain. Madrid's attractiveness comes in its ability to flawlessly integrate history and modernity, providing tourists with unique experiences and a strong appreciation for the city's dynamic personality.

Overview of neighborhoods and districts

Madrid, the capital of Spain, is a city noted for its rich history, breathtaking architecture, and dynamic culture. The city is split into various neighborhoods and districts, each with a particular character and attractions. Here is an overview of some of the crucial areas and communities of Madrid:

1. Puerta del Sol: Located in the center of the city, Puerta del Sol is not only a significant transit hub but also a vibrant

area full of stores, restaurants, and prominent buildings. It is home to the iconic clock tower, the emblem of Madrid, the Bear, and the Strawberry Tree monument. Puerta del Sol is a vibrant gathering spot and a fantastic starting point for exploring the city.

2. Gran Vía: Known as the "Spanish Broadway," Gran Vía is Madrid's major street. This lively boulevard has theaters, shops, restaurants, and beautiful architecture. It is a center of activity, particularly at night, when the neon lights brighten the roadway. Gran Vía is a retail wonderland and provides a bustling ambiance day and night.

3. Malasaña: Malasaña is a popular area recognized for its alternative and bohemian feel. It is distinguished by tiny alleyways, colorful buildings, and a busy nightlife scene. This region was in the vanguard of the cultural movement known as the Movida Madrileña in the 1980s. Today, Malasaña is a famous destination for art galleries, antique

boutiques, quirky pubs, and live music venues.

4. Chueca: Chueca is Madrid's LGBTQ+ district and is recognized for its welcoming and energetic vibe. It is a busy district with fashionable pubs, clubs, and restaurants catering to various clientele. Chueca is famed for its yearly Pride events, which draw guests from all over the globe. It's a friendly community that celebrates diversity and boasts a busy nightlife.

5. Lavapiés: Lavapiés is a cosmopolitan and bohemian area that shows Madrid's variety. It is home to a vast immigrant community and provides diverse cultures, languages, and cuisines. Lavapiés is noted for its multicultural eateries, bustling street art culture, and alternative music venues. Exploring the small lanes of Lavapiés gives a look into Madrid's heterogeneous fabric.

6. Retiro: Retiro is a neighborhood that surrounds the spectacular Parque del

Buen Retiro, a vast park replete with gardens, fountains, and the famed Crystal Palace. This region emanates elegance and calm, with broad streets, upmarket stores, and gorgeous architecture. Retiro is also home to numerous prominent museums, notably the Prado Museum, making it the city's cultural heart.

7. Salamanca: Salamanca is one of Madrid's most wealthy areas, famed for its luxury stores, high-end restaurants, and magnificent residential structures. It is a trendy area with large boulevards, exquisite buildings, and designer boutiques. Salamanca is a sanctuary for shopping fans and provides a polished and elegant environment.

8. La Latina: La Latina is a lovely area famed for its traditional tapas eateries, ancient architecture, and busy street market, El Rastro. It is an excellent destination for residents and visitors alike to walk around the market on Sunday and indulge in tasty tapas. La

Latina has a bustling environment, especially in the evening when the clubs and restaurants come to life.

These are only a handful of the numerous neighborhoods and districts that make up the unique fabric of Madrid. Each district has its charm, sights, and tastes, enabling visitors to experience the city's dynamic culture from diverse angles. Exploring these districts gives a broader grasp of Madrid's history, architecture, food, and and native way of life. Whether you're meandering through the vibrant alleys of Malasaña, enjoying the cultural events in Lavapiés, or indulging in posh shopping in Salamanca, each area provides a different vibe and an opportunity to explore Madrid's hidden jewels.

9. Barrio de las Letras: Barrio de las Letras, also known as the Literary Quarter, is a district that pays tribute to some of Spain's most prominent authors, including Cervantes and Lope de Vega. Stroll through its small

alleyways covered with literary quotations and visit the lovely bookstores, art galleries, and traditional pubs. This area emits a creative and intellectual air.

10. La Castellana: La Castellana is a significant boulevard and commercial sector that runs through the center of Madrid. It is home to spectacular buildings, business offices, and luxury hotels. Along this vast road, you'll discover prominent structures such as the Gate of Europe towers and the Santiago Bernabeu Stadium, home of the famed Real Madrid football team.

11. Lavapiés: Lavapiés is a cosmopolitan area recognized for its dynamic and varied vibe. It is a melting pot of cultures, mixing traditional Spanish shops, ethnic eateries, and unusual art venues. Lavapiés organizes cultural events and festivals annually, reflecting the neighborhood's diversity and creative energy.

12. Chamberí: Chamberí is a residential area known for its exquisite 19th-century buildings and peaceful streets. It provides a calmer and more residential feel than the crowded city core. Chamberí is recognized for its attractive squares, small markets, and picturesque cafés. Take a leisurely walk along its tree-lined avenues and enjoy the neighborhood's ageless beauty.

13. Madrid Río: Madrid Río is a renovated waterfront district along the banks of the Manzanares River. It provides a vast green area, excellent for outdoor activity and relaxation. Explore the parks, gardens, and walking routes, or hire a bike and travel along the river. Madrid Río also has contemporary architectural masterpieces, such as the Matadero cultural complex, which holds exhibits, concerts, and events.

14. El Paseo del Arte (Art Walk): El Paseo del Arte is an area that comprises three world-class art museums: the Prado Museum, the Thyssen-

Bornemisza Museum, and the Reina Sofía Museum. This art-centric neighborhood is a heaven for art enthusiasts, featuring an extensive array of treasures spanning from classical to modern art. Spend a day immersed in the works of great painters such as Velázquez, Picasso, and Dalí.

Tourists may experience the city's rich history, culture, and unique atmosphere by touring Madrid's many neighborhoods and districts. From the lively energy of Malasaña to the elegance of Salamanca, each neighborhood provides a distinct viewpoint on Madrid's vivid personality. So, travel beyond the well-known sights and embrace the local areas to completely immerse yourself in the heart of this magnificent city.

Local customs and etiquette

Madrid, the capital of Spain, is a city noted for its rich history, breathtaking architecture, and dynamic culture. The city is split into various neighbourhoods and districts, each with particular characteristics and attractions. Here is an overview of some of the crucial neighbourhoods and districts of Madrid:

1. Puerta del Sol: Located in the centre of the city, Puerta del Sol is not only a significant transit hub but also a vibrant area full of stores, restaurants, and renowned buildings. It is home to the iconic clock tower and the emblem of Madrid, the Bear and the Strawberry Tree monument. Puerta del Sol is a vibrant gathering spot and a fantastic starting point for exploring the city.

2. Gran Vía: Known as the "Spanish Broadway," Gran Vía is Madrid's major street. This lively boulevard has theatres, shops, restaurants, and beautiful

architecture. It is a centre of activity, particularly at night, when the neon lights brighten the roadway. Gran Vía is a retail wonderland and provides a bustling ambience day and night.

3. Malasaña: Malasaña is a popular area recognized for its alternative and bohemian feel. It is distinguished by tiny alleyways, colourful buildings, and a busy nightlife scene. This region was in the vanguard of the cultural movement known as the Movida Madrileña in the 1980s. Today, Malasaña is a famous destination for art galleries, antique boutiques, quirky pubs, and live music venues.

4. Chueca: Chueca is Madrid's LGBTQ+ district and is recognized for its welcoming and energetic vibe. It is a busy district with fashionable pubs, clubs, and restaurants catering to various clientele. Chueca is famed for its yearly Pride events, which draw guests from all over the globe. It's a pleasant community that celebrates

diversity and boasts a busy nightlife.

5. Lavapiés: Lavapiés is a cosmopolitan and bohemian area that shows Madrid's variety. It is home to a huge immigrant community and provides diverse cultures, languages, and cuisines. Lavapiés is noted for its multicultural eateries, bustling street art culture, and alternative music venues. Exploring the small lanes of Lavapiés gives a look into Madrid's heterogeneous fabric.

6. Retiro: Retiro is a neighbourhood that surrounds the spectacular Parque del Buen Retiro, a vast park replete with gardens, fountains, and the famed Crystal Palace. This region emanates elegance and calm, with broad streets, upmarket stores, and gorgeous architecture. Retiro is also home to numerous prominent museums, notably the Prado Museum, making it the city's cultural heart.

7. Salamanca: Salamanca is one of Madrid's most wealthy areas, famed for

its luxury stores, high-end restaurants, and magnificent residential structures. It is a trendy area with large boulevards, exquisite buildings, and designer boutiques. Salamanca is a sanctuary for shopping fans and provides a polished and elegant environment.

8. La Latina: La Latina is a lovely area famed for its traditional tapas eateries, ancient architecture, and busy street market, El Rastro. It is an excellent destination for residents and visitors alike to walk around the market on Sunday and indulge in tasty tapas. La Latina has a bustling environment, especially in the evening when the clubs and restaurants come to life.

These are only a handful of the numerous neighbourhoods and districts that make up the unique fabric of Madrid. Each district has its charm, sights, and tastes, enabling visitors to experience the city's dynamic culture from diverse angles. Exploring these districts gives a broader grasp of

Madrid's history, architecture, food, and native way of life. From the busy Puerta del Sol to the fashionable streets of Malasaña and Chueca, from the cosmopolitan atmosphere of Lavapiés to the elegance of Retiro and Salamanca, and from the traditional tapas restaurants of La Latina to the famed Gran Vía, each area adds to the vivid tapestry of Madrid.

9. Huertas (Barrio de las Letras): Huertas, also known as Barrio de las Letras, is a neighbourhood rich in literary tradition. It was previously home to some of Spain's most distinguished authors, including Miguel de Cervantes and Lope de Vega. The streets of Huertas are covered with lines from notable literary works, and the region is studded with bookshops, literary cafés, and cultural institutes. It is a lovely area that highlights Madrid's literary legacy.

10. Lavapiés: Lavapiés, recognized for its cosmopolitan ambience, is a neighbourhood with vitality and

innovation. It is a melting pot of many cultures, with a bustling mix of eateries providing food from across the globe, vivid street art, and a flourishing independent art scene. Lavapiés is also renowned for its colourful street festivals and cultural events, making it a vibrant and dynamic neighbourhood to explore.

11. Chamberí: Chamberí is a residential area with a serene and sophisticated ambience. It is highlighted by its broad tree-lined streets, magnificent architecture, and well-preserved old buildings. Chamberí provides a gentler side of Madrid, with beautiful cafés, boutique stores, and local markets. It is a neighbourhood that enables tourists to experience the local way of life and escape the rush and bustle of the city centre.

12. Madrid Río: Madrid Río is a contemporary and recreational area that spans the banks of the Manzanares River. It provides a pleasant retreat from

the metropolitan scene, with wide green spaces, walking and cycling pathways, and leisure places. Madrid Río is great for outdoor sports, picnics, or leisurely walking along the riverbanks. It gives a tranquil getaway in the centre of the metropolis.

Exploring the many neighbourhoods and districts of Madrid enables tourists to discover the city's varied personalities, immerse themselves in its history and culture, and appreciate the unique flavours of each place. Whether you're seeking historical sites, bustling nightlife, cultural immersion, or calm getaways, Madrid's districts offer something for every traveller's tastes and interests.

Safety tips and precautions

When visiting Madrid, it's crucial to emphasize safety and take the required steps to guarantee a pleasant and secure vacation. Here are some safety guidelines to bear in mind when touring the city:

1. Be careful in busy locations: Madrid is lively, particularly in major tourist sites. Stay mindful of your surroundings, particularly in busy markets, public transit, and prominent attractions. Be aware of pickpockets and constantly check your valuables, especially wallets, purses, and electronic gadgets.

2. Use dependable transportation: Madrid has a well-developed public transit system, including buses, metro, and trains. Opt for licensed taxis or utilize approved ride-hailing services for transportation. If you prefer walking, stay on the well-lit, crowded streets, particularly at night.

3. Stay knowledgeable about local legislation: Familiarize yourself with local laws, regulations, and traditions. This includes having emergency contact numbers, understanding local

transportation restrictions, and honouring cultural customs. Adhere to local limitations or recommendations, especially during public rallies or protests.

4. Secure your lodgings: Choose reliable and secure hotels throughout your trip. Look for rooms that have high ratings and are situated in safe districts. Ensure your hotel room has sufficient security elements, such as solid locks and a safe to protect your valuables.

5. Carry minimum cash and use cards cautiously: Carrying just the essential amount of cash and avoiding showing huge quantities of money in public is preferable. Use credit or debit cards for purchases wherever feasible, but be careful when entering your PIN or revealing your card information. Keep your cards in a safe location and contact your bank or credit card issuer in advance of your vacation intentions.

6. Stay connected and informed: Have a dependable method of communication, such as a cell phone with local emergency numbers stored. Stay updated about local news and any possible safety recommendations or warnings issued during your stay. Consider registering with your embassy or consulate for any travel advisories or updates.

7. follow local conventions and dress modestly: Madrid is a diverse city, yet it's crucial to follow local customs and cultural standards. Dress modestly, especially while visiting religious places, and be conscious of local customs and sensibilities.

8. Avoid excessive alcohol intake: While Madrid has a dynamic nightlife scene, it's crucial to drink sensibly and be cautious of your alcohol usage. Excessive drinking might impair judgment and make you more sensitive to possible threats.

9. Travel with the company: Tour the city with partners whenever feasible. Travelling in groups may boost safety and repel possible dangers. If you're going out at night, staying in well-lit and busy locations is advised.

Remember, these safety suggestions are basic principles, and it's always a good idea to be educated and adapt to unique conditions. By being vigilant, taking essential measures, and applying common sense, you may have a safe and pleasurable time while experiencing the bustling city of Madrid.

Section 3.2: Top Attractions in Madrid

Prado Museum

The Prado Museum, formally known as the Museo Nacional del Prado, is one of the world's most famous and recognized art museums. Located in Madrid, Spain, the museum is home to a significant collection of European art, with a particular concentration on Spanish treasures. It is considered a must-visit location for art fans and cultural vacationers.

Here is some significant information about the Prado Museum:

1. History and Architecture: The Prado Museum was created in 1819 by King Ferdinand VII and opened to the public in 1819. The museum building is a marvel of art architect Juan de Villanueva created. The neoclassical construction contains magnificent halls, wide galleries, and a stunning central courtyard, providing an exquisite and harmonious atmosphere for showcasing art.

2. Art Collection: The Prado Museum features over 8,000 paintings and over 700 sculptures. The collection runs from the 12th to the 19th century, embracing

many creative trends and styles. The museum's principal concentration is Spanish art, containing pieces by notable painters such as Francisco Goya, Diego Velázquez, and El Greco. However, it also has famous works by Italian, Flemish, and Dutch painters, such as Titian, Rubens, and Rembrandt.

3. Highlights: The Prado Museum holds many important and acclaimed artworks. Some of the most famous masterpieces include "Las Meninas" by Velázquez, a captivating portrait of the Spanish royal family; "The Third of May 1808" by Goya, depicting a sombre scene from the Spanish War of Independence; and "The Garden of Earthly Delights" by Hieronymus Bosch, a captivating triptych filled with symbolism and surreal imagery. These artworks, among many others, illustrate the museum's outstanding collection and aesthetic importance.

4. Temporary exhibits and Educational Programs: Besides its permanent

collection, the Prado Museum often presents temporary exhibits, providing visitors with the chance to examine certain subjects, artists, or eras in more depth. These exhibits typically draw worldwide notice and bring unique insights into art. The museum also provides educational programs, guided tours, and workshops for all ages, making it a fascinating and enlightening experience for visitors of all backgrounds.

5. Prado Museum Extension: In recent years, the Prado Museum experienced a considerable extension with the addition of the Jerónimos Building. This addition enlarged the museum's exhibition area, allowing for a more thorough presentation of its collection. The new building features contemporary architecture while smoothly blending with the previous structure.

Visiting the Prado Museum gives a unique chance to immerse oneself in art and experience prominent painters' creativity throughout history. Its extraordinary collection, architectural splendour, and devotion to encouraging art appreciation make it a cultural treasure and a must-visit site for everyone interested in understanding the rich artistic legacy of Spain and Europe.

Royal Palace of Madrid

The Royal Palace of Madrid, commonly known as the Palacio Real de Madrid, is a vast and luxurious monument that serves as the official house of the Spanish royal family. Located in the centre of Madrid, the palace is one of the city's most famous and frequented attractions. Here is a summary of the Royal Palace and its significance:

1. History and Architecture: Construction of the Royal Palace started in 1738 and was finished in 1764, but it was not formally opened until 1850. The

palace was created in the Baroque and Neoclassical architectural styles by prominent architects, including Filippo Juvarra and Francesco Sabatini. Its majestic façade, embellished with sculptures and elaborate decorations, symbolizes the majesty and magnificence of the Spanish monarchy.

2. Layout and Interior: The Royal Palace is a massive edifice covering over 130,000 square meters and 3,400 rooms. While only a tiny section of these rooms is exposed to the public, visitors may tour the luxurious staterooms, royal chambers, banquet halls, and the stunning Royal Armory, which displays a massive collection of antique weapons and armour. The palace interiors are filled with exquisite decorations, complex tapestries, rare artwork, and opulent furniture, exhibiting Spain's royal lineage and aesthetic riches.

3. Changing of the Guard: One of the prominent sights of the Royal Palace is the Changing of the Guard ritual. This

event occurs every Wednesday and Saturday at noon in front of the palace's main entrance, the Puerta del Príncipe. Visitors may watch the accuracy and splendour of this classic military rite as troops march in formation, escorted by a military band.

4. grounds & Surroundings: The Royal Palace is bordered by exquisite grounds, known as the Campo del Moro and Sabatini Gardens, which give a tranquil and picturesque refuge from the busy city. The Campo del Moro is a huge park with rich flora, groomed grass, and peaceful ponds. The Sabatini Gardens, named after the palace's architect, present a beautiful and symmetrical environment with fountains, hedges, and sculptures, affording excellent castle views.

5. Cultural Events and Exhibitions: Besides being a royal dwelling, the palace also acts as a location for ceremonial ceremonies, state banquets, and cultural events. It routinely holds

concerts, exhibits, and other cultural events, allowing visitors to explore the palace in diverse circumstances and enjoy a range of creative and musical acts.

Visiting the Royal Palace of Madrid enables guests to immerse themselves in the grandeur and history of the Spanish monarchy. The palace's architectural beauty, elaborately embellished interiors, gorgeous gardens, and cultural activities make it a must-see site for anyone interested in learning the royal past of Spain and experiencing the richness of a bygone period.

Retiro Park

Retiro Park, formally known as Parque del Buen Retiro, is a stunning urban park in Madrid, Spain's centre. It is the city's major green area and a popular leisure place for residents and visitors alike. Retiro Park offers a calm getaway from the hectic city streets and provides a serene location for relaxation, leisure activities, and cultural discovery. Here is an overview of Retiro Park and its attractions:

1. History and Architecture: Originally belonging to the Spanish crown, Retiro Park was opened to the public in the late 19th century. The park is noted for its historical importance and has architectural components that represent several times. The most noteworthy architectural element is the Palacio de Cristal, a spectacular glass pavilion created in the late 19th century. Other prominent constructions are the Monument to Alfonso XII, the Velázquez Palace, and the Retiro Gate.

2. Natural Beauty: Retiro Park is recognized for its natural beauty, containing huge green fields, rich gardens, and stunning views. Visitors may wander along the tree-lined pathways, rest on the groomed lawns, or picnic in the quiet surroundings. The

park is also home to a big artificial lake, where tourists may hire rowboats and enjoy leisurely sea trips.

3. Gardens and Monuments: Retiro Park has various well-maintained gardens and renowned monuments. The Rosaleda Garden is a paradise for rose fans, containing a collection of more than 4,000 rose plants. The Jardín de Vivaces is a bright garden featuring various colourful and unusual plants. The park also has essential monuments and sculptures, such as the Fountain of the Fallen Angel and the statue of King Alfonso XII, which gives panoramic views of the park and its surroundings.

4. Cultural and Recreational Activities: Retiro Park provides tourists with a choice of cultural and recreational activities. The park regularly holds art exhibits, concerts, and outdoor plays, offering a venue for artists and musicians to display their abilities. Fitness lovers may use the park's jogging routes, bicycle lanes, and

outdoor workout facilities. Additionally, specialized places for athletic activity include football, basketball, and roller skating.

5. El Palacio de Velázquez and El Palacio de Cristal: Retiro Park is home to two outstanding exhibition spaces: El Palacio de Velázquez and El Palacio de Cristal. El Palacio de Velázquez holds contemporary art exhibits featuring works by national and international artists. El Palacio de Cristal, a famous glass edifice, presents temporary exhibits and installations, frequently showcasing modern art and sculptures.

Retiro Park's blend of natural beauty, historical sites, cultural events, and recreational options make it a favourite destination for inhabitants and tourists. Whether you want to take a leisurely stroll, have a picnic, visit art exhibits, or just find a tranquil space to rest, Retiro Park offers a serene and lovely hideaway in the centre of Madrid.

Puerta del Sol

Puerta del Sol, meaning "Gate of the Sun," is one of Madrid, Spain's most dynamic and recognizable squares. Located in the middle of the city, it is a major transit hub and a popular gathering area for residents and visitors alike. Puerta del Sol possesses considerable historical and cultural value and provides a bustling environment with several attractions. Here is an overview of Puerta del Sol and its highlights:

1. Historical Significance: Puerta del Sol has played a key role in the history of Madrid. In the past, it functioned as one of the city's gates, marking the eastern entrance. The area has seen several notable events, including political marches, festivities, and historic announcements. It is regarded as the kilometre zero, from which all important Spanish highways are calculated.

2. Iconic Landmarks: The square is home to numerous renowned landmarks, which are must-see attractions for tourists. One of the most iconic icons of Madrid, situated in Puerta del Sol, is the Bear and the Strawberry Tree monument. It features a bear reaching for a strawberry tree, signifying the city's coat of arms. Another noteworthy sight is the clock tower atop the Casa de Correos (Post Office Building), which shows the customary New Year's Eve countdown and draws big crowds during the festivities.

3. Shopping and Commercial Area: Puerta del Sol is a lively commercial area with many shops, boutiques, and department stores. It is a popular location for shopping, with a mix of well-known worldwide brands and local speciality businesses. The area is also home to the famed El Corte Inglés department store, a prominent Spanish retail business.

4. Gastronomic Delights: The area around Puerta del Sol is lined with classic Spanish taverns, cafés, and restaurants where tourists may indulge in exquisite Spanish food. From tasting tapas to enjoying regional delicacies, plenty of alternatives suit every appetite. Enjoying a meal or a cool drink at one of the outdoor terraces while people-watching is a classic experience in Puerta del Sol.

5. Cultural and Social Hub: Puerta del Sol is a dynamic social hub, drawing people from all walks of life. Street performers, singers, and painters regularly entertain guests with their abilities, contributing to the colourful environment. The area also annually holds cultural events and festivals, including concerts, art exhibits, and holiday celebrations.

6. Connectivity and Accessibility: Puerta del Sol is a major transportation centre in Madrid, with multiple metro and bus lines meeting in the area. This makes it

readily accessible from many city sections, making it a suitable starting place for visiting Madrid's attractions.

Puerta del Sol's central position, historical importance, lively atmosphere, and diversity of activities make it a must -visit site for everyone experiencing Madrid. It combines history, culture, shopping, cuisine, and entertainment, offering tourists a real flavour of the city's dynamic atmosphere and rich legacy.

Plaza Mayor

Plaza Mayor, or "Main Square," is a beautiful architectural jewel and one of the most prominent sites in Madrid, Spain. Situated in the heart of the city's historic core, Plaza Mayor is a dynamic and busy area that goes back to the 17th century. It has enormous historical, cultural, and social value, drawing residents and visitors. Here is an outline of Plaza Mayor and its highlights:

1. Historical Significance: Plaza Mayor has seen various noteworthy events. Originally erected during Habsburg, it functioned as a marketplace, holding bullfights, coronations, royal festivities, and even public executions. Over the years, it has been a significant meeting place for Madrileños and a focus of social and cultural activity.

2. Architectural Beauty: The square's architectural architecture is a Spanish Baroque and Herrerian style masterwork. The homogeneity of the area's surrounding structures provides a beautiful and symmetrical ambience. The facades contain balconies, architectural embellishments, and beautiful paintings, reflecting the grandeur of the past. The most famous architectural feature is the Casa de la Panadería, a historic house with murals representing mythical themes and historical events.

3. Plaza Mayor Arcades: Plaza Mayor is famed for its famous arcades that skirt the area's circumference. These arcades include a variety of stores, cafés, and restaurants where tourists may enjoy a meal or buy souvenirs. The arcades have a pleasant ambience and give shade during hot summer days, making them a popular area for leisure and people-watching.

4. monument of Philip III: At the heart of Plaza Mayor sits a monument of King Philip III on horseback. The monument pays respect to the king who launched the creation of the area. It is a prominent feature of the area and typically acts as a gathering spot for residents and tourists.

5. Cultural Events & Festivals: Plaza Mayor remains a thriving cultural hub, holding many events and festivals annually. It is a place for street performances, concerts, art displays, and traditional celebrations. The area comes alive during Christmas, New

Year's Eve, and San Isidro, Madrid's patron saint's day when it is covered with decorations and hosts colourful events.

6. Terraces & outside Dining: The restaurants and cafés in Plaza Mayor provide outside seating on the square, letting tourists enjoy the bustling ambience while indulging in wonderful Spanish food. Dining on one of the terraces gives a unique experience, with views of the plaza and its colourful ambience.

Plaza Mayor's rich history, spectacular architecture, bustling atmosphere, and cultural importance make it an important destination for Madrid tourists. Whether you want to appreciate the architectural splendour, eat a meal in a lovely café, or immerse yourself in the cultural activities, Plaza Mayor provides a riveting experience that reflects the spirit of Madrid's history and present.

Gran Via

Gran Vía, or "Great Way," is one of Madrid's most renowned and busiest thoroughfares. It is a dynamic and energetic street that spans the city centre, combining commerce, entertainment, and architectural magnificence. Gran Vía is an iconic emblem of Madrid's modernism and has become linked with the city's dynamic vibe. Here is a summary of Gran Vía and its highlights:

1. Architectural Marvels: Gran Vía is noted for its spectacular architectural marvels that line the Boulevard. The buildings feature various architectural styles, including Art Nouveau, Art Deco, and Neo-Mudéjar. Some famous structures are the Metropolis Building, Telefonica Building, and Edificio Carrión (known as the Capitol Building), which boasts a rooftop sign that has become an iconic emblem of Gran Vía.

2. Shopping Paradise: Gran Vía is a shopper's paradise, featuring many shops, boutiques, and department stores. You may discover worldwide fashion labels, local designers, and prominent Spanish merchants here. Gran Vía caters to all shopping inclinations and budgets, from apparel and accessories to cosmetics and gadgets.

3. Entertainment Hub: Gran Vía is recognized for its bustling entertainment scene. The street has various theatres, cinemas, and live music venues. You may witness a Broadway-style musical at one of the renowned theatres, enjoy a movie in a historic cinema, or experience live music performances ranging from flamenco to current genres. Gran Vía comes alive at night with the bustle of nightlife and entertainment alternatives.

4. Culinary Delights: Gran Vía provides a broad choice of eating alternatives, from traditional Spanish cuisine to

cosmopolitan delicacies. You may discover charming cafés, tapas bars, fashionable restaurants, and rooftop terraces where you can enjoy gastronomic delicacies. Whether searching for a quick snack or a gourmet dining experience, Gran Vía offers something to satisfy every taste.

5. Landmark Hotels: Gran Vía is home to numerous renowned hotels that have played a key role in the city's hospitality sector. These hotels not only provide exquisite rooms but also act as architectural jewels. Staying at one of these famous hotels affords a unique chance to immerse yourself in the history and elegance of Madrid.

6. Street Life and People-watching: Walking along Gran Vía enables you to see the colourful street life of Madrid. The Boulevard is usually packed with activity, from inhabitants going about their daily routines to visitors visiting the city. Enjoy a leisurely walk, see the different populations, and imbibe in the

lively ambience that distinguishes Gran Vía.

Gran Vía is an emblem of Madrid's multicultural and contemporary nature. Its gorgeous architecture, busy shops, dynamic entertainment scene, and gastronomic options make it an exciting destination for travellers. Whether you are seeking retail therapy, cultural events, or just want to soak in the colourful ambience of the city, Gran Vía is a must-visit boulevard that captures the essence of Madrid.

Mercado de San Miguel

Mercado de San Miguel, or San Miguel Market, is a famous food market in the centre of Madrid, Spain. It is a gourmet wonderland that provides a tremendous gastronomic experience for guests. Housed in a stunning iron and glass building, the market mixes classic beauty with a contemporary touch. Here is an overview of Mercado de San

Miguel and its highlights:

1. Historical Significance: Mercado de San Miguel has a long history from 1916. Initially, It was a wholesale food market, but it has recently become a popular gourmet market. The market has undergone repairs to retain its architectural legacy, including its unique iron framework, artistic glasswork, and elegant entrance.

2. Gourmet Delights: The market is recognized for its vast array of gourmet food and drink products. It contains a variety of vendors and kiosks, each exhibiting a delectable selection of Spanish delights. From fresh seafood, meats, and cheeses to tapas, pastries, and wines, tourists can taste the flavours of Spain in one area. The market is a heaven for food enthusiasts, featuring a blend of classic and modern cuisine.

3. Tapas & Small Plates: One of the features of Mercado de San Miguel is its

tapas culture. The market is a fantastic venue to indulge in the Spanish habit of consuming tiny plates of exquisite food. You may enjoy a broad choice of tapas, including Spanish favourites such as jamón ibérico (cured ham), croquetas, tortilla española (Spanish omelette), and pintxos (Basque-style tapas on bread).

4. Local and International Fare: Mercado de San Miguel displays Spanish food and international delicacies. Alongside typical Spanish booths, you will discover merchants providing foods from diverse culinary traditions, including sushi, oysters, Mediterranean specialities, and more. This variety makes the market a melting pot of flavours, catering to varied tastes and inclinations.

5. Socializing and environment: The market's bustling and colourful atmosphere adds to its attraction. The bustling energy, the perfume of freshly cooked food, and the clinking of glasses create a sociable environment that inspires guests to socialize and enjoy

their gastronomic discoveries. The market is a gathering centre for residents and visitors. It is a great site to immerse yourself in the local culture and interact with other food aficionados.

6. Events and seminars: Mercado de San Miguel routinely conducts culinary events, seminars, and tastings, offering chances for visitors to connect with local cooks, learn about Spanish food, and increase their culinary talents. These activities give a greater knowledge of the culinary culture and provide an engaging experience inside the market's colourful environment.

Mercado de San Miguel is a must-visit place for food enthusiasts and those wanting a real flavour of Madrid's gastronomic culture. With its vast choice of culinary goods, convivial ambience, and historical charm, the market gives a unique chance to indulge in Spanish sensations, discover new tastes, and make memorable gastronomic memories.

Section 3.3: Beyond the Mainstream

Lesser-known sites and hidden treasures

Madrid, the dynamic city of Spain, is recognized for its famous monuments and cultural attractions. However, the city also conceals lesser-known attractions and hidden gems that provide a look into its rich past and unique charm. Exploring these off-the-beaten-path jewels may deliver a distinct and genuine Madrid experience. Here are some lesser-known sights and hidden gems in Madrid:

1. El Capricho Park: Tucked away in the city's northeastern section, El Capricho Park is a hidden paradise that provides

solitude and natural beauty. This park is a lesser-known jewel with magnificent gardens, exquisite pavilions, and a lovely lake. It's a perfect area to escape the hectic metropolis and enjoy a calm walk among beautiful foliage.

2. Temple of Debod: Situated near the Royal Palace, the Temple of Debod is a surprising ancient Egyptian temple in the centre of Madrid. Donated by Egypt to Spain, this 2,200-year-old temple was demolished and reassembled in Madrid. It gives a rare chance to discover ancient Egyptian architecture and has a museum showing items from ancient Egypt.

3. Sorolla Museum: Tucked away in the posh area of Chamberí, the Sorolla Museum is devoted to the works of famous Spanish artist Joaquín Sorolla. The museum is housed in the artist's old home and shows his paintings, sculptures, and personal things. It delivers an intimate and immersive journey into the lives and work of this

remarkable painter.

4. Chamberí Ghost Metro Station: Chamberí Ghost Station is a treasure for history and metro fans. Located on Line 1 of the Madrid Metro, this abandoned station has been kept in its original 1919 Art Nouveau form. Visitors may travel back in time and experience the historic ticket hall, platforms, and exhibitions representing the Madrid Metro's history.

5. Conde Duque Cultural Center: Housed in former military barracks, the Conde Duque Cultural Center provides a variety of cultural events, exhibits, and performances. It displays modern art and offers concerts, film screenings, and theatrical events. The complex also has attractive courtyards and gardens where guests may rest and enjoy the tranquil ambience.

6. San Antonio de la Florida Hermitage: Located beyond the city centre, the San Antonio de la Florida Hermitage is a hidden gem noted for its beautiful

paintings by Francisco Goya. The hermitage includes Goya's renowned fresco, "The Miracle of Saint Anthony," visitors may examine the fine intricacies and brilliance of Goya's work in this lesser-known cultural jewel.

7. Debod Viewpoint: Near the Temple of Debod, a lesser-known viewpoint gives panoramic views of Madrid's cityscape. From this vantage point, tourists may enjoy beautiful perspectives of the city, including the Royal Palace and Casa de Campo Park. It's a perfect site to snap breathtaking images and experience the beauty of Madrid from a fresh viewpoint.

Exploring these lesser-known places and hidden gems in Madrid enables tourists to explore beyond the well-trodden roads and uncover the city's hidden attractions. From quiet parks to cultural institutions and historical buildings, these off-the-beaten-path jewels give a unique and rewarding experience, affording a greater grasp of Madrid's history, art, and local culture.

Unique dining experiences and local cuisine

Madrid is a gastronomic wonderland that provides a wealth of unique dining experiences and thriving native cuisine. From classic cuisine to new inventions, the city features a diversified culinary scene that appeals to every taste. Here is an overview of the distinctive dining experiences and local food in Madrid:

1. Tapas Culture: Madrid is famed for its tapas culture, where tiny plates of delectable nibbles are designed to be shared and savoured with a drink. Tapas bars and pubs may be located throughout the city, giving a vast choice of delicious alternatives. From traditional meals like patatas bravas (fried potatoes with spicy sauce) and gambas al ajillo (garlic shrimp) to inventive contemporary adaptations, tapas give a fantastic chance to taste various flavours in one meal.

2. Mercados (Food Markets): Madrid's food markets, such as Mercado de San Miguel and Mercado de San Antón, are gastronomic havens where tourists can immerse themselves in the local cuisine. These markets display a vivid mix of fresh fruit, meats, seafood, and gourmet products. You may indulge in a range of meals from various kiosks, relishing anything from Iberian ham and artisanal cheeses to seafood paella and oysters.

3. Cocido Madrileño: Cocido Madrileño is a substantial and traditional Madrid stew suitable for colder months. It comprises chickpeas, different meats (such as hog, beef, and chicken), veggies, and spices. The meal is traditionally served in three courses: the broth, followed by the chickpeas and veggies, and lastly, the meats. Cocido Madrileño is a famous comfort meal that reflects Madrid's strong tastes and culinary traditions.

4. Bocadillo de Calamares: A iconic Madrid street snack, the bocadillo de Calamares is a sandwich packed with crunchy deep-fried squid rings. This simple but tasty snack is popular among residents and visitors alike. You may find it at many taverns and food vendors, particularly in the city centre. Pair it with a cool beer for the ultimate combo.

5. Churros and Chocolate: Indulging in churros and chocolate is a treasured Madrid custom. Head to classic churrerías, such as Chocolatería San Ginés, and experience freshly cooked churros coated in thick, creamy hot chocolate. It's a lovely delicacy that can be eaten for breakfast, a lunchtime snack, or even late at night after a night out.

6. Gastronomic Markets and Gastrobars: Madrid has various gastronomic markets and gastro bars that provide new and contemporary interpretations of classic food. These venues bring together brilliant chefs and culinary

artists, giving a platform for imaginative and high-quality eating experiences. From molecular gastronomy to fusion cuisine, these places exhibit the cutting-edge side of Madrid's culinary culture.

7. Vermouth and Aperitivo Culture: Joining locals for vermouth and aperitivo is a common social activity in Madrid. Many restaurants and taverns offer a broad range of vermouth, a fortified wine flavoured with herbs and spices, followed by small snacks known as aperitivos. It's a terrific opportunity to chill and mingle while enjoying Madrid's colourful and convivial environment.

8. Gastronomic Festivals: Madrid celebrates many gastronomic festivals annually, honouring diverse parts of its culinary culture. One prominent event is the Gastrofestival, which takes place in January and February. It displays various culinary activities, including special meals, cooking courses, tastings, and food-themed exhibits. It's a chance to sample Madrid's food in a joyful and

immersive atmosphere.

9. classic Tascas & Mesones: Tascas and mesones are classic taverns and cafes that provide an insight into Madrid's gastronomic past. These places frequently feature a rustic and intimate ambience, providing classic foods with genuine tastes. Here, you may enjoy foods like robust stews, grilled meats, and handmade sweets, all cooked using time-honoured traditions and methods.

10. Fusion Cuisine: Madrid's culinary sector promotes innovation and fusion, resulting in a dynamic fusion cuisine. Many restaurants merge classic Spanish tastes with influences from other cuisines, providing unique and intriguing gastronomic experiences. From Asian-inspired tapas to Mediterranean fusion meals, you may go on a culinary adventure that mixes varied tastes and methods.

11. Vermut de Grifo: Madrid has a distinct passion for vermouth, and one unique experience is experiencing vermut de grifo, which refers to vermouth served on tap. Several pubs and bodegas in Madrid sell vermouth directly from the tap, delivering a fresh and genuine flavour. It's a great way to taste this popular drink in its purest form.

12. Gastrotours and Food Experiences: For those wishing to dig further into Madrid's culinary culture, gastrotours and food experiences are a terrific alternative. These guided excursions take you through various areas, presenting you with hidden culinary treasures, traditional restaurants, and local delicacies. You may go on a tapas tour, a wine-tasting adventure, or even join in cookery workshops to master the secrets of Spanish food.

13. Local Wine & Artisan Beer: Madrid's gastronomic pleasures are typically matched by outstanding local wines and

artisan brews. You may tour the wine bars and bodegas offering a range of Spanish wines, including those from the adjacent Ribera del Duero and Rioja areas. Additionally, the craft beer industry in Madrid has been expanding, with microbreweries and beer bars providing a broad choice of artisanal beers to complement your eating experiences.

14. Traditional Pastries and Sweets: Madrid features a range of traditional pastries and sweets worth discovering. From the classic churros and chocolate to the exquisite tartan de Santiago (almond cake), rosquillas (doughnuts), and torrijas (a Spanish variant of French toast), you can fulfil your sweet taste with these wonderful sweets. Remember to visit the city's famed pastry shops and bakeries to indulge in these scrumptious sweets.

15. Food Markets Beyond the City Center: While Mercado de San Miguel is a prominent food market, Madrid offers

other small markets worth seeing. Mercado de Vallehermoso, Mercado de San Ildefonso, and Mercado de la Paz are just a few examples. These markets provide a more local and genuine experience, where you can discover fresh produce, handmade items, and a range of gastronomic choices away from the hectic tourist districts.

Exploring the distinct eating experiences and local cuisine in Madrid enables you to taste this lively city's flavours, customs, and innovations. From traditional meals to fusion masterpieces and secret taverns to contemporary gourmet pleasures, Madrid's culinary scene invites you to embark on a gastronomic adventure that will leave you with wonderful memories and a greater appreciation for Spanish food.

Flamenco shows and nightlife recommendations

Madrid is famed for its bustling nightlife and deep-rooted relationship with flamenco, the passionate and expressive Spanish dance genre. If you want to enjoy the dynamic nightlife and witness the mesmerizing art of flamenco, Madrid has lots to offer. Here is an overview of flamenco concerts and nightlife tips in Madrid:

1. Flamenco Shows: Madrid is home to various tablaos, places devoted to exhibiting flamenco acts. These presentations include expert dancers, impassioned singers, and great guitarists who join to create an electric environment. Some well-known tablaos are Casa Patas, Corral de la Morería, and Cardamomo Tablao Flamenco, where you can watch real and strong flamenco performances that exhibit the talent and passion of this enchanting dance genre.

2. Peñas Flamencas: Peñas Flamencas are flamenco clubs or organizations where aficionados assemble to admire and enjoy flamenco. These tiny venues typically hold performances by rising performers and provide a more traditional and intimate atmosphere to enjoy flamenco. Peña Flamenca El Güito and Peña Flamenca La Platería are famous instances where you may watch real and passionate flamenco performances.

3. Flamenco Dance Classes: If you're intrigued by the art of flamenco, why not attend a dance lesson in Madrid? Many dance schools and academies offer flamenco courses for all levels, enabling you to master this mesmerizing dance form's fundamental moves and rhythms. Taking a lesson gives a hands-on experience and a greater knowledge of the precise footwork and expressive motions that make flamenco so appealing.

4. Tapas and Bar Hopping: Madrid's evening is only complete with partaking in the city's tapas culture and bar hopping scene. The city is littered with innumerable pubs and taverns where you may eat excellent tapas combined with your favourite beverages. Explore areas like La Latina, Malasaña, and Huertas, where you'll discover an abundance of pubs providing a broad range of tapas and a vibrant ambience that lingers late into the night.

5. Cocktail pubs and Rooftop Terraces: Madrid features a bustling cocktail culture, with various pubs and clubs providing inventive and beautifully made drinks. Some businesses, such as Salmon Guru, Del Diego, and 1862 Dry Bar, are recognized for their mixology skills and sophisticated ambience. Additionally, the city is peppered with rooftop terraces that give panoramic skyline views while enjoying cool beverages and a classy ambience.

6. Live Music Venues: Madrid is a mecca for live music fans, with venues catering to a broad spectrum of musical genres. You may discover various live music alternatives, from jazz clubs like Café Central and Populart to rock venues like El Sol and Siroco. These venues generally showcase local and international acts, creating a lively and exciting nightlife experience.

7. Late-Night Flamenco Jams: For a unique and spontaneous flamenco experience, check for late-night flamenco jams known as "juergas." These unexpected meetings generally occur in tiny flamenco bars called peñas, when musicians and dancers get together for an informal session of improvisation and cooperation. These jirgas give a real and honest peek into the lyrical heart of flamenco.

When visiting flamenco events and Madrid's nightlife, preparing ahead is vital since certain venues demand reservations, particularly for popular tablaos and peñas. Whether you prefer to immerse yourself in the intensity of flamenco shows or enjoy the dynamic ambiance of tapas restaurants and live music venues, Madrid's nightlife scene provides an exciting and unique experience that highlights the city's vitality and creative character.

Day trips and excursions from Madrid

Being positioned in the centre of Spain, Madrid is a good starting place for exciting day trips and excursions to explore the surrounding areas. From ancient sites to stunning landscapes, there are many possibilities for day excursions from Madrid. Here are some prominent places worth considering:

1. Toledo: Known as the "City of Three Cultures," Toledo is a UNESCO World Heritage site and a wonderful day trip

from Madrid. Its rich history is reflected in its architectural masterpieces, notably the beautiful Toledo Cathedral, Alcázar of Toledo, and Synagogue of Santa María la Blanca. Stroll through the small lanes, see the old city walls, and appreciate the panoramic views of the Tagus River from the Mirador del Valle.

2. Segovia: Segovia is recognized for its spectacular Roman aqueduct, which is a witness to its historic history. Marvel at the well-preserved aqueduct, tour the fairytale-like Alcázar of Segovia and see the majestic Segovia Cathedral. Don't miss the chance to eat the region's delicacy, cochinillo (suckling pig), in one of the local restaurants.

3. Ávila: With its well-preserved medieval walls, Ávila provides a voyage back in time. Walk around the walls to experience panoramic views of the city, see the majestic Ávila Cathedral, and tour the Convent of Saint Teresa, devoted to the great Spanish mystic and writer. The city is especially famed for

its scrumptious Yemas de Ávila, a traditional dessert from egg yolks.

4. El Escorial: El Escorial is home to the majestic Royal Monastery of San Lorenzo de El Escorial, a UNESCO World Heritage site. This architectural marvel functioned as a palace, monastery, and tomb for the Spanish kings. Explore the stately halls, view the huge library, and meander around the gorgeous grounds surrounding the property.

5. Aranjuez: Aranjuez is a lovely town famed for its gorgeous Royal Palace and Gardens, which is also a UNESCO World Heritage site. Explore the sumptuous interiors of the palace, wander through the large gardens with their fountains and lush foliage, and see the Casa del Labrador, a beautiful royal home nestled within the grounds.

6. Cuenca: Cuenca is notable for its unusual hanging homes (Casas Colgadas) on the cliff brink. Explore the old city centre, also a UNESCO World

Heritage site, and see the stunning views from the San Pablo Bridge. Take the chance to see the Museum of Abstract Art, presenting an exceptional collection of modern artwork.

7. Valle de los Caídos: The Valle de los Caídos, or the Valley of the Fallen, is a magnificent memorial commemorating those who perished during the Spanish Civil War. The complex features a basilica cut into the slope and a towering crucifix located in the Sierra de Guadarrama. Explore the basilica's beautiful interior and take in the sombre mood of this ancient place.

These are just a few examples of the various day trips and excursions you might go on from Madrid. Whether you're interested in history, architecture, natural beauty, or cuisine, the surrounding areas offer many activities that will enhance your vacation to Spain's dynamic capital city.

Chapter Four

Experiencing Spanish Culture

Understanding Spanish traditions and festivals

Spanish customs and festivals are strongly anchored in the country's rich cultural past and distinct regional identities. From vivid street processions to boisterous celebrations, Spain provides a myriad of customs and festivals that exhibit its history, religion, culture, and community spirit. Here are some noteworthy Spanish customs and festivals:

1. Semana Santa (Holy Week): Semana Santa is one of Spain's most prominent religious traditions, practised in numerous cities and villages around the nation. It takes place in the week leading

up to Easter Sunday. It comprises sombre processions commemorating events from the Passion of Christ. Clad in traditional robes, participants carry holy sculptures through the streets accompanied by eerie music and incense.

2. La Tomatina: La Tomatina is a unique and renowned celebration in Buñol near Valencia. It occurs on the final Wednesday of August when participants participate in a gigantic tomato battle. People assemble in the streets, and truckloads of tomatoes are tossed, producing a vibrant and colourful sight that draws both residents and visitors.

3. Feria de Abril: The Feria de Abril is a bright and happy event celebrated in Seville approximately two weeks following Semana Santa. It involves a week of festivities packed with flamenco music and dancing, traditional costumes, horse parades, carnival attractions, and excellent Andalusian food. The fairgrounds are decked with

colourful tents (casetas) where people congregate to chat and enjoy the festivities.

4. San Fermín and the Running of the Bulls: San Fermín, celebrated in Pamplona from July 6th to 14th, is recognized for the famed "Running of the Bulls" (encierro). Participants sprint ahead of a bunch of bulls through the tight alleyways of the city, demonstrating their courage and agility. The celebration also features traditional music, dancing, and bullfights in the city's bullring.

5. La Feria de Málaga: La Feria de Málaga is a colourful celebration celebrated in August that honours the city's past. It encompasses a week of flamenco, traditional music, dance, colourful processions, fireworks, and street acts. The event generates a lively environment when residents and tourists come together to celebrate the Andalusian culture.

6. La Fiesta de San Juan: La Fiesta de San Juan, observed on June 23rd, is a statewide holiday honouring the summer solstice. Bonfires are lit on beaches and in public spaces, and people come to celebrate with music, dancing, fireworks, and traditional ceremonies. It is thought that leaping over the campfire brings good luck and cleanses the soul.

7. La Feria del Caballo: La Feria del Caballo is an annual horse fair in Jerez de la Frontera in Andalusia. It celebrates the region's equestrian heritage, horsemanship demonstrations, and dressage contests. The fair also incorporates flamenco music and dancing, bullfights, and an abundance of Andalusian cuisine and wine.

8. Fallas de Valencia: Fallas is a unique celebration held in Valencia from March 15th to 19th. It includes the fabrication and presentation of gigantic, elaborate paper-mâché sculptures called fallas. These sculptures are eventually

destroyed in magnificent bonfires known as "La Cremà," accompanied by pyrotechnics and music.

These are only a few instances of the various customs and festivals that span the diverse areas of Spain. Each festival represents its individual locality's specific cultural character and local customs, offering a look into the lively and varied fabric of Spanish traditions. Participating in these festivals enables tourists to immerse themselves in the country's rich history and discover the authentic essence of Spanish culture. From religious processions to boisterous street celebrations, these customs and festivals unite communities and create a memorable and engaging experience for residents and tourists alike.

It's worth mentioning that Spain also celebrates numerous national holidays, including:

1. Día de la Hispanidad (National Day): Celebrated on October 12th, this festival honours Christopher Columbus' entrance into the Americas and the union of the Spanish-speaking nations.

2. Fiesta Nacional de España (National Day of Spain): Observed on October 12th, this day honours the Spanish Constitution and the nation's unity.

3. Día de la Constitución (Constitution Day): Celebrated on December 6th, this day honours the ratification of the Spanish Constitution in 1978.

4. Día de la Inmaculada Concepción (Feast of the Immaculate Conception): Celebrated on December 8th, this religious feast celebrates the belief in the immaculate conception of the Virgin Mary.

In addition to these national holidays, each area in Spain has distinct local festivals and customs that exhibit its cultural history. Whether it's the strong passion for flamenco in Andalusia, the colourful Catalan festivities in Catalonia, or the Basque country's particular festivals, Spain's rich tapestry of customs and festivals provides a completely immersive and captivating experience.

It's essential to remember that festival dates and particular events may change from year to year, so it's best to check the local tourist websites or contact a trusted source for the most up-to-date information before organizing your visit.

Embracing Spanish customs and participating in festivals helps you to interact with the country's unique cultural fabric, connect with its people, and create memorable memories. Whether you see the magnificent processions of Semana Santa, join the wild street celebrations of La Tomatina, or experience the true charm of local festivities, you're sure to be intrigued by the richness and variety of Spanish customs and festivals.

Gastronomic delights

Madrid, the capital city of Spain, is a gourmet paradise that provides a fascinating assortment of culinary delights. From classic Spanish delicacies to inventive fusion cuisine, Madrid's culinary culture is broad, dynamic, and likely to delight any pallet. Here are some culinary delicacies you may taste in Madrid:

1. Tapas: Madrid is famed for its tapas culture. Head to the lively areas of La Latina, Malasaña, and Huertas, where you'll discover countless pubs selling an assortment of scrumptious tapas. From traditional favourites like patatas bravas (fried potatoes with spicy sauce) and tortilla española (Spanish omelette) to more experimental alternatives like gambas al ajillo (garlic shrimp) and croquetas (croquettes), tapas enable you to taste a range of flavours in one sitting.

2. Cocido Madrileño: Cocido Madrileño is a hearty traditional stew that originated in Madrid. Made with chickpeas, vegetables, and different types of meat (such as hog, beef, and chicken) and served in many courses, it is a meal that symbolizes the rich culinary tradition of the city. Don't miss the chance to indulge in this soothing and flavoursome meal, particularly during winter.

3. Bocadillo de Calamares: A characteristic Madrid dish, the bocadillo de Calamares is a simple but delicious sandwich stuffed with crunchy fried squid rings. Head to the busy Plaza Mayor or the colourful Mercado de San Miguel to sample this renowned street cuisine. The combination of delicate squid, crusty bread, and a touch of lemon is a wonderful joy.

4. Churros with Chocolate: Indulge your sweet taste with a typical Madrid treat—churros con chocolate. These

deep-fried dough pastries are served hot and crispy, frequently coated with sugar, and accompanied by a thick and creamy hot chocolate dip. This combo is a must -try in Madrid, savoured as a morning treat or an afternoon snack.

5. Pimientos de Padrón: Pimientos de Padrón are little green peppers from Padrón in Galicia, a region in northwest Spain. These mild peppers are frequently cooked till blistered and sprinkled with sea salt. It's a popular tapas dish that adds a taste and a sense of excitement to your gastronomic trip.

6. Cochinillo Asado: Cochinillo asado, or roasted suckling pig, is a delicacy profoundly established in Spanish cuisine. You may discover restaurants specializing in this classic cuisine in Madrid, delivering soft and luscious roasted piglets with crispy skin. It's a must-try for meat lovers seeking a genuine and flavoursome eating experience.

7. Gastro Markets: Madrid has various gastro markets, including Mercado de San Miguel, Mercado de San Antón, and Mercado de San Ildefonso. These colourful markets provide a broad choice of food booths and sellers where you may try local and foreign cuisine. From fresh seafood and artisanal cheeses to gourmet tapas and craft brews, these markets create a dynamic and exciting ambience for food enthusiasts.

8. Pastries and Desserts: Madrid's pastry shops and bakeries are heaven for dessert connoisseurs. Indulge in exquisite sweets like the creamy and flaky ensaimada (a spiral-shaped pastry), the sweet and crumbly tart de Santiago (almond cake), or the famous churros with various fillings and toppings.

While these are only a few examples, Madrid's culinary industry provides a variety of possibilities to explore. Traditional meals that pay respect to Madrid's gastronomic culture offer many possibilities to explore. From classic cuisine that pays respect to the city's rich past to creative concoctions that reflect the inventiveness of current chefs, there is something for everyone. Here are a few more culinary treats you may savour in Madrid:

9. Mercado de San Miguel: Mercado de San Miguel is a historic food market near Plaza Mayor. Here, you may immerse yourself in a culinary paradise filled with vendors providing a broad choice of gourmet tapas, fresh seafood, cured meats, handmade cheeses, and delightful sweets. It's a fantastic spot to engage in a gastronomic experience and enjoy a range of cuisines under one roof.

10. Vermouth & Aperitivos: Madrid has a thriving aperitivo culture, and sipping vermouth or a refreshing aperitif is a common practice. Join the locals at their favourite taverns and pubs, and sip a drink of vermouth accompanied by tiny snacks like olives, cheese, and anchovies. This pre-meal practice is a

lovely way to whet your appetite and enjoy the city's friendly vibe.

11. Fusion food: Madrid's eating culture embraces fusion food, merging traditional Spanish tastes with other influences. Explore unique restaurants that put a new take on classic meals, integrating ingredients and methods from throughout the globe. From Asian-inspired tapas to Mediterranean fusion concoctions, these culinary journeys will surprise and satisfy your taste buds.

12. Cocina de Vanguardia: Madrid is famed for its avant-garde food, frequently referred to as "cocina de vanguardia." This innovative and creative cooking style challenges traditional Spanish cuisine's limits. You may indulge in a gourmet trip at Michelin-starred restaurants that provide painstakingly created tasting menus offering creative dishes that demonstrate the culinary skills of famous chefs.

13. Vermicelli Stew (Sopa de Fideos): Sopa de Fideos is a warm and savoury traditional soup prepared with vermicelli noodles, vegetables, and occasionally meat or fish. It's a popular dish in Madrid, particularly during winter, delivering a warm and gratifying gastronomic experience.

14. Craft Beer and Gin pubs: Madrid has experienced growth in the craft beer and gin sector, with various pubs and breweries providing a broad range of locally made beers and artisanal gins. Explore the colourful districts of Malasaña and Lavapiés, where you'll discover snug taverns selling artisan beers and fashionable gin bars offering a myriad of gin and tonic variations.

15. Wine Tastings: Spain is famous for its superb wines, and Madrid is no exception. Attend a wine-tasting lesson or visit one of the city's wine bars to try a selection of Spanish wines, including the famed Rioja, Ribera del Duero, and Priorat. Immerse yourself in the rich

wine culture of Spain and experience the unique tastes and characteristics of its numerous wine regions.

From traditional delicacies to cutting-edge cuisine, Madrid's culinary pleasures are guaranteed to please even the most sophisticated food aficionados. Whether you prefer to indulge in classic cuisine, discover novel tastes, or just immerse yourself in the exciting ambiance of food markets and tapas bars, Madrid provides a gastronomic experience guaranteed to impact your taste buds.

Wine and culinary tours in Barcelona and Madrid

Wine and culinary excursions in Barcelona and Madrid provide a pleasant overview of the region's gourmet gems and wine culture. These trips give an immersive experience where you can indulge in excellent cuisine, sip fine wines, and acquire insights into Spain's culinary traditions and wine-making skills. Here's what you can anticipate from wine and cuisine excursions in Barcelona and Madrid:

1. Wine Tastings: Wine tastings are a fundamental feature of these trips, enabling you to enjoy a range of Spanish wines. In Barcelona, you may explore the famed wine areas of Penedès, Priorat, or Alella, where you'll have the chance to sample magnificent wines, including sparkling Cava, strong reds, and crisp whites. In Madrid, you may visit the adjacent wine areas of Ribera del Duero, La Mancha, or Rueda, recognized for their high-quality wines. Experienced sommeliers or local experts take you through the tasting process, giving their expertise about the wines' characteristics, production processes, and match ideas.

2. Vineyard trips and Winery Tours: Wine tours frequently include trips to

vineyards and wineries, offering behind-the-scenes insight into the wine-making process. You may tour the verdant vineyards, learn about grape farming, and experience the wine-making techniques practised in the area. Guided tours at vineyards enable you to view the cellars, learn about the ageing process, and comprehend the complexities of wine production. These visits give a unique chance to meet with the winemakers, ask questions, and increase your understanding of the art of wine-making.

3. Food Pairings & Culinary Experiences: Wine and culinary excursions go hand in hand, enabling you to experience the ideal synergy between food and wine. You'll experience traditional Spanish foods and gourmet cuisine meticulously combined with the wines you taste. From tapas and pintxos to elaborate tasting meals, these trips emphasize the regional culinary peculiarities and exhibit the different tastes of Spanish food. Expert chefs and sommeliers lead you

through the matching process, explaining the ideas underlying the pairings and expanding your awareness of how tastes interact.

4. Cooking lessons: Some trips provide immersive cooking lessons where you can discover Spanish food's secrets from skilled chefs. These hands-on activities walk you through making classic meals, including paella, gazpacho, or tapas. You'll learn about the dishes' materials, methods, and cultural importance while experiencing the delight of producing your own culinary creations. After the lesson, you'll sample the foods you cooked and the well-chosen wines.

5. Cultural and Historical Insights: Wine and culinary tours concentrate on the sensory elements of food and wine and give cultural and historical insights into the location. Expert guides provide tales and anecdotes about the local customs, culinary history, and the historical importance of wine production. You'll

better grasp the link between wine, gastronomy, and the cultural fabric of Barcelona and Madrid.

6. Visits to Local Markets and Gastronomic Hotspots: These tours often include visits to bustling local markets, such as Barcelona's La Boqueria or Madrid's Mercado de San Miguel, where you can witness the vibrant atmosphere and discover a variety of fresh produce, cheeses, meats, and other culinary delights. You may also visit secret gourmet hotspots and old pubs recognized for their original cuisine, enabling you to immerse yourself in the local food scene.

Wine and culinary trips in Barcelona and Madrid blend cultural immersion, gastronomic discovery, and wine enjoyment. Whether you're a wine connoisseur, a cuisine lover, or someone seeking a unique vacation experience, these trips provide an excellent chance to revel in Barcelona and Madrid's tastes, scents, and traditions. Here are a few additional characteristics of wine and cuisine excursions in these bustling cities:

7. Gourmet Experiences: Wine and culinary tours frequently include gourmet experiences where you may dine at Michelin-starred restaurants or famous local eateries. These places demonstrate the ingenuity and culinary ability of recognized chefs who merge classic cuisines with contemporary methods. You'll get to sample expertly designed meals with great wines, delivering a unique gourmet experience.

8. Regional specialities: Barcelona and Madrid have their own specialities you can try throughout the trips. In Barcelona, you may taste seafood specialities like paella de marisco (seafood paella), fideuà (noodle paella), or suquet de peix (Catalan fish stew). Madrid, on the other hand, is famed for delicacies like cocido madrileño (Madrid -style stew), callos a la madrileña (Madrid-style tripe), and sopa de ajo

(garlic soup). These gastronomic treats showcase the distinct tastes and culinary traditions of each location.

9. Wine Education: Wine and culinary excursions give educational opportunities to learn about the world of wine. You'll acquire insights into Spain's numerous grape varietals, wine-making processes, and wine regions. Experts and sommeliers will lead you through the tasting process, helping you refine your taste, comprehend wine qualities, and enjoy the intricacies of each sip. You'll learn about the elements determining wine quality and experience the variety of Spanish wines.

10. Cultural Immersion: Beyond the food and wine, these trips allow immersing oneself in the local culture. You'll mingle with enthusiastic winemakers, chefs, and locals firmly attached to their culinary heritage. You could tour scenic vineyards, visit ancient wine-making estates, or wander around the busy streets of Barcelona and Madrid,

uncovering hidden jewels and enjoying the dynamic atmosphere.

11. Customization and Flexibility: Wine and culinary trips may be personalized to fit your tastes and interests. Whether you want a private trip, a group adventure, or a particular concentration on certain wine areas or culinary characteristics, tour operators may construct an itinerary that meets your tastes. They can accommodate food needs, design unique activities, and give customized attention, ensuring your trip is a delightful and memorable experience.

Wine and culinary excursions in Barcelona and Madrid combine gourmet pleasures, wine appreciation, cultural insights, and immersive experiences. Whether you're a wine aficionado, a cuisine enthusiast, or just someone who likes the better things in life, these trips give you an unparalleled chance to uncover the rich culinary legacy and wine culture of these dynamic towns. So, be ready to tickle your taste buds, uncork the finest wines, and go on a gastronomic trip you'll love for years.

Art and Architecture

Art and architecture in Barcelona and Madrid are famous internationally for their rich history, distinctive styles, and significant artists. Both towns possess many cultural treasures, ranging from ancient Roman buildings to modernist masterpieces. Here's an overview of the art and architectural scene in Barcelona and Madrid:

Barcelona:

1. Modernist Architecture: Barcelona is linked with modernist architecture, pioneered by the visionary architect Antoni Gaudí. His greatest designs, such as the entrancing Sagrada Família, the whimsical Park Güell, and the stunning Casa Batlló, demonstrate a mix of

organic forms, brilliant colours, and detailed details. Exploring these architectural wonders gives an insight into Gaudí's creative universe and his distinct vision of Catalan modernism.

2. Gothic Quarter: Barcelona's Gothic Quarter, known as the Barri Gòtic, is a maze of small alleys and squares filled with Gothic architecture. The magnificent Barcelona Cathedral, with its majestic façade and elaborate interior, is a tribute to the city's medieval heritage. Walking through this ancient district exposes hidden jewels like the Plaça del Rei and the Palau de la Generalitat, showing the majesty of Gothic architecture.

3. Picasso Museum: Barcelona pays tribute to one of the most significant painters of the 20th century, Pablo Picasso. The Picasso Museum exhibits an extensive collection of his early works, offering insight into his creative growth and showing his exceptional genius. From his early years through his

avant-garde experimentation, the museum gives a full trip through Picasso's creative history.

Madrid:

1. Prado Museum: The Prado Museum is a treasure trove of art featuring an extraordinary collection of European classics. It displays paintings by prominent painters like Velázquez, Goya, El Greco, and Bosch. From the eerie "Las Meninas" to Goya's forceful "The Third of May 1808," the museum gives a wonderful overview of Spanish art history and is a must-visit for art fans.

2. Royal Palace of Madrid: The Royal Palace of Madrid is a majestic architectural masterpiece that serves as the official home of the Spanish Royal Family. Its sumptuous interiors, decorated with extravagant decorations, fine furnishings, and valuable artworks, depict the grandeur of the Spanish monarchy. The palace provides guided tours, enabling visitors to see its grand

halls, the Royal Armoury, and the wonderfully kept grounds.

3. Reina Sofía Museum: The Reina Sofía Museum is devoted to modern art and is home to a significant collection of Spanish and foreign works. It holds Picasso's renowned masterwork, "Guernica," and a comprehensive collection of artworks from the surrealist movement, including works by Salvador Dalí and Joan Miró. The museum gives a thought-provoking overview of modern and contemporary art.

4. Retiro Park: While not primarily devoted to art, Retiro Park is a huge green sanctuary in the centre of Madrid that features amazing sculptures and architectural aspects. The Crystal Palace, an iron and glass edifice, accommodates modern art exhibits. At the same time, the monument to Alfonso XII and the Fountain of the Fallen Angel gives a touch of grandeur to the park's aesthetic attractiveness.

Barcelona and Madrid provide an intriguing combination of architectural styles, from the ancient Gothic Quarter of Barcelona to the modernist marvels of Gaudí and the grandeur of Madrid's royal palaces. Both towns' art museums have outstanding collections spanning centuries, presenting a thorough overview of Spanish and worldwide art. Whether you're an architectural aficionado or an art lover, experiencing the creative legacy of Barcelona and Madrid is a trip that will inspire and enchant you at every step.

Flamenco and live music experiences

Flamenco and live music experiences in Barcelona and Madrid give an exciting immersion into Spanish music and dance's deep rhythms and passionate performances. From the fierce footwork to the poignant lyrics, these events exhibit the rich cultural legacy of Spain. Here's an overview of Flamenco and live music in Barcelona and Madrid:

Barcelona:

1. Flamenco Shows: Barcelona boasts a strong Flamenco culture, where you can see enthralling performances in tiny locations. Flamenco presentations showcase amazing dancers, expert guitarists, and heartfelt singers that bring this classic art form to life. The raw passion, precise footwork, and haunting melodies create an extraordinary experience that brings you to the heart of Spanish culture.

2. Tablao Flamenco: Tablao Flamenco venues in Barcelona give a specialized location for experiencing true Flamenco. These small settings enable you to get up close and personal with the artists, immersing yourself in the intensity and emotion of the dance. Renowned Flamenco performers regularly grace

the stages, exhibiting mastery of this emotive art style.

3. Live Music Venues: Barcelona has a lively live music scene catering to varied musical interests. From jazz clubs to traditional Catalan music venues, you may discover diverse concerts across the city. These venues present local and international performers, giving a unique chance to experience live music in an intimate and atmospheric atmosphere.

Madrid:

1. Flamenco Shows at Tablaos: Madrid is regarded as one of the birthplaces of Flamenco, and the city offers a multiplicity of famous Flamenco tablaos (venues). These tables showcase great Flamenco performances involving skilled dancers, musicians, and vocalists. The deep emotions, powerful footwork, and soul-stirring voices create an immersive experience that embodies the essence of Flamenco.

2. Corral de la Morería: Corral de la Morería is one of Madrid's most renowned Flamenco venues, noted for its excellent concerts and long history. Established in 1956, it has hosted great Flamenco performers and continues to produce top-notch performances. The location provides an intimate atmosphere where you can watch the enchanting talent of Flamenco up close.

3. Live Music in La Latina and Malasaña: The areas of La Latina and Malasaña in Madrid are renowned for their active nightlife and live music scene. You'll discover a range of taverns, clubs, and small places where local artists play live music covering diverse genres. Whether you like jazz, rock, or traditional Spanish music, these areas provide a dynamic environment to watch live performances.

4. Café de Chinitas: Café de Chinitas is another legendary Flamenco establishment in Madrid that has been delighting audiences since 1970. It highlights Flamenco in an intimate

atmosphere, including brilliant performers who fascinate with their superb dance, heartfelt singing, and expressive guitar playing. The venue's rich history and passionate performances provide an exquisite Flamenco experience.

Flamenco and live music experiences in Barcelona and Madrid allow one to observe Spanish music and dance's raw intensity and cultural relevance. Whether you prefer to immerse yourself in the fiery rhythms of Flamenco or enjoy live performances in other musical genres, these experiences will leave you with lasting recollections of the rich music scene in these dynamic cities. So, be ready to stomp your feet, clap your hands, and be touched by the passionate music and compelling performances Barcelona and Madrid offer.

CHAPTER FIVE

PRACTICAL INFORMATION

Essential Spanish phrases and useful vocabulary
When travelling to Barcelona and Madrid, it's helpful to know some essential Spanish phrases and useful vocabulary to navigate your way around and interact with locals. Here are a few key phrases and words that will come in handy:

1. Greetings and Basic Phrases:
   - Hello: Hola
   - Good morning: Buenos días
   - Good afternoon/evening: Buenas tardes
   - Good night: Buenas noches
   - Please: Por favor
   - Thank you: Gracias
   - You're welcome: De nada
   - Excuse me: Disculpe
   - I'm sorry: Lo siento

- Yes: Sí
- No: No
- Goodbye: Adiós

2. Introductions:
- What is your name?: ¿Cómo te llamas? (informal) / ¿Cómo se llama? (formal)
- My name is...: Me llamo...
- Nice to meet you: Mucho gusto
- How are you?: ¿Cómo estás? (informal) / ¿Cómo está? (formal)
- I'm fine, thank you: Estoy bien, gracias

3. Directions and Transportation:
- Where is...?: ¿Dónde está...?
- How do I get to...?: ¿Cómo llego a...?
- Bus station: Estación de autobuses
- Metro station: Estación de metro
- Train station: Estación de tren
- Airport: Aeropuerto
- Left: Izquierda
- Right: Derecha
- Straight ahead: Todo recto
- Map: Mapa
- Ticket: Billete

4. Ordering Food and Drinks:
   - I would like...: Me gustaría...
   - Menu: Menú
   - Water: Agua
   - Coffee: Café
   - Beer: Cerveza
   - Wine: Vino
   - Breakfast: Desayuno
   - Lunch: Almuerzo
   - Dinner: Cena
   - Bill: Cuenta

5. Shopping:
   - How much does it cost?: ¿Cuánto cuesta?
   - Can I try it on?: ¿Puedo probármelo?
   - Do you have this in a different size/colour?: ¿Tiene esto en otra talla/color?
   - I'm just browsing: Solo estoy mirando
   - Cash: Efectivo
   - Credit card: Tarjeta de crédito

Remember, speaking a few Spanish phrases will be greatly appreciated by locals and can enhance your overall experience. Even if your pronunciation isn't perfect, the willingness to communicate in their language shows respect and can lead to more meaningful interactions. So, don't hesitate to practice these essential phrases and embrace the opportunity to engage with the locals in Barcelona and Madrid.

Money matters

Regarding money concerns in Barcelona and Madrid, it's necessary to know the local currency, payment methods, and basic banking information. Here are some crucial considerations to bear in mind:

1. Currency: - The official currency in both Barcelona and Madrid is the Euro (€). Keeping some Euros on hand for minor expenditures and establishments that may not take credit cards is good.

2. Cash and Cards: - Credit and debit

cards are generally accepted in most locations, including hotels, restaurants, and stores. Visa and Mastercard are the most often accepted cards, followed by American Express and Diners Club. - It's a good idea to use cash and cards for convenience. ATMs (known as "cajeros automáticos") are freely accessible throughout both cities, enabling you to withdraw cash as required.

3. Exchange Rates: - Exchange rates might fluctuate. Therefore, verifying the rates at banks or authorized exchange agencies is essential. Avoid converting money at unregistered enterprises since they may provide poor rates or participate in fraud.

4. Banking Hours: - Banks in Barcelona and Madrid normally operate from Monday through Friday, with most branches open from 8:30 AM to 2:00 PM. Some bigger branches may provide longer afternoon hours on select weekdays. It's advisable to examine the exact banking hours of your selected

bank branch.

5. Tipping: - Tipping at restaurants and cafés is common in Spain but is not as widespread as in some other countries. Generally, giving a 10% tip is considered courteous and appreciated. In higher-end restaurants, a significantly higher tip may be warranted.

6. Value Added Tax (VAT): - Spain levies a Value Added Tax (VAT) known as "IVA" to most products and services. The regular rate is 21%, while lower rates of 10% and 4% apply to some commodities such as food, literature, and medical supplies. Prices listed in shops and restaurants frequently include VAT.

7. Safety and Security: - Like any large metropolis, you must be aware of your possessions and apply common sense while handling money. Be aware of pickpockets, particularly in popular tourist locations, and consider utilizing a money belt or a lockable travel wallet to

keep your belongings safe.

8. Travel Insurance: - It is advisable to obtain travel insurance that covers medical bills, trip cancellation, and lost or stolen possessions. Check with your insurance carrier to ensure you have appropriate coverage for your trip to Barcelona and Madrid.

By familiarizing yourself with these money concerns, you may easily manage financial transactions and have a hassle-free vacation in Barcelona and Madrid. Remember to advise your bank or credit card provider of your trip intentions to enable seamless card use overseas, and constantly watch your things to protect the safety of your money and personal stuff.

Communication and Internet access

Communication and internet connection in Barcelona and Madrid are typically stable, making it simple to remain connected throughout your vacation. Here's everything you need to know:

1. Mobile Network Coverage: - Both cities offer good mobile network coverage, assuring robust signal strength for calls, messages, and mobile data. Major providers in Spain include Movistar, Vodafone, Orange, and Yoigo. Check with your home cell service provider for overseas roaming plans, or try obtaining a local SIM card for more cost-effective possibilities.

2. Wi-Fi Availability: - Wi-Fi is readily accessible in Barcelona and Madrid. Many hotels, cafés, restaurants, and public venues provide free Wi-Fi connectivity for clients. Look for signage or contact the staff for the Wi-Fi password if necessary.

3. Internet Cafes: - If you need access to mobile data or require a more dependable internet connection, you may locate internet cafes in both cities.

These places give computers with an internet connection for a price, enabling you to surf the web, check emails, or make online calls.

4. Messaging applications: - Using messaging applications such as WhatsApp, Telegram, or Skype may be a handy and cost-effective method to remain in contact with family and friends back home. These programs let you conduct voice and video conversations, exchange messages, and share material through an internet connection.

5. Public Telephones: - While the usage of public telephones has reduced with the advent of mobile phones, you can still find them in several locations in Barcelona and Madrid. They generally need money or phone cards, which may be bought at convenience shops or kiosks.

6. Language Barrier: - Spanish is the official language in both cities; however,

English is commonly spoken in tourist areas, hotels, and restaurants. However, acquiring a few basic Spanish words to aid with conversation is always beneficial, particularly in more local or non-touristy places.

7. Navigation Apps: - To traverse the cities and find your way around, use navigation applications like Google Maps or Citymapper. These applications include precise instructions, public transit routes, and anticipated trip times, letting you navigate the streets and public transportation systems smoothly.

8. Emergency Services: - In case of crises, the universal emergency number in Spain is 112, which links you to police, medical, or fire services. The operators typically know English and may help you in numerous scenarios.

Remember to be aware of data consumption if you depend on mobile data to remain connected since roaming costs may apply depending on your cell service provider. Additionally, always take the required steps to safeguard your personal information and utilize secure networks while accessing sensitive information online.

With the availability of mobile networks, Wi-Fi hotspots, and communication applications, keeping connected and traversing the cities of Barcelona and Madrid is straightforward, enabling you to make the most of your trip experience.

Health and safety tips

When going to Barcelona and Madrid, it's crucial to consider your health and safety to guarantee a smooth and pleasurable journey. Here are some health and safety recommendations to keep in mind:

1. Travel Insurance: - Before your journey, ensure sure you have travel

insurance that covers coverage for medical emergencies, trip cancellations, and lost or stolen possessions. Familiarize yourself with the policy and have the relevant papers with you.

2. Medical Facilities: Barcelona and Madrid have excellent medical facilities and hospitals. In case of a medical emergency, phone the local emergency number (112) or seek help at the closest hospital or healthcare institution. If feasible, it's important to bring any essential prescription drugs with you and have a copy of your medical documents.

3. immunizations: - Check with your healthcare practitioner or travel clinic before your trip to ensure you are current on regular immunizations. They may also suggest extra immunizations depending on your travel intentions.

4. Hygiene: - Practice proper hygiene by washing your hands frequently with soap and Water or using hand sanitiser

when soap is unavailable. Carry hand sanitiser with you, particularly when visiting busy locations or before dining.

5. Tap Water: - Tap Water in both Barcelona and Madrid is typically safe to drink. However, if you prefer bottled Water, it is easily available.

6. Sun Safety: Both cities endure bright and warm weather, especially during summer. Protect yourself from the sun by using sunscreen with a high SPF, a hat, sunglasses, and lightweight clothes. Stay hydrated by drinking lots of Water throughout the day.

7. Personal Safety: - Like any other large city, stay cautious of your surroundings and take essential steps to secure your valuables. Avoid displaying precious goods and lock critical papers, such as your passport, in a hotel safe. Be vigilant of pickpockets, especially in busy tourist areas and on public transit.

8. Emergency Services: - Familiarize

yourself with the local emergency numbers: 112 for general situations, 091 for the police, and 061 for medical emergencies. Keep these numbers accessible in case of any unforeseen emergencies.

9. COVID-19 Considerations: - Stay updated about the newest COVID-19 rules and limitations in Barcelona and Madrid. Follow local restrictions for mask-wearing, social separation, and other protective measures. Stay current on travel warnings and restrictions and be prepared to comply with any health and safety standards in place.

Before your trip, it's always good to read the latest travel warnings and advice from your country's government or official travel websites. By remaining educated, taking appropriate measures, and prioritizing your health and safety, you can have a wonderful and worry-free trip to Barcelona and Madrid.

Local customs and etiquette to be aware of

When visiting Barcelona and Madrid, one must educate oneself about the local traditions and etiquette to guarantee a courteous and enjoyable experience. Here are some crucial traditions and etiquette considerations to bear in mind:

1. Greetings: - A handshake is the typical greeting when meeting someone for the first time. In more casual circumstances, friends and acquaintances may greet each other with a kiss on both cheeks.

2. Punctuality: - Being timely while attending meetings, social functions, or appointments is normal. Arriving a few minutes early is considered nice.

3. eating Times: - Spaniards often have a later eating schedule compared to certain other nations. Lunch is often between 1:30 PM and 3:00 PM, while supper is usually served from 8:30 PM onwards. Adjusting to these meal hours

might let you fully appreciate the local eating culture.

4. Dining Etiquette: - When eating out, it is conventional politeness to wait for the host or the waiter to take you to your seat. Remember that tipping is valued but less prevalent than in some other nations. A 10% tip is considered courteous.

5. Dress Code: - Barcelona and Madrid are cosmopolitan cities. Dressing modestly and politely while visiting churches, religious sites, or more traditional neighbourhoods is essential. Revealing apparel may be judged unacceptable in such contexts.

6. Language: - Learning a few simple Spanish words may go a long way in demonstrating respect for the local culture. Even if your Spanish is weak, making an effort to greet, thank, and participate in basic conversation in Spanish will be welcomed by locals.

7. Respect for Siesta: - In certain smaller towns and areas, you may discover the customary siesta period in the early afternoon. During this time, businesses and stores may temporarily shut. It's crucial to be cognizant of this habit and schedule your actions properly.

8. Queuing: - Spaniards usually respect queuing and waiting in line. Wait your turn when queuing for public transit, attractions, or services. Avoid pushing or jumping the line.

9. Personal Space: - Spaniards often enjoy personal space. Only standing too near to people if the occasion dictates it, such as in crowded public transit.

10. Respect for Local Customs and Symbols: - Respect local norms, traditions, and symbols. For example, while visiting religious places, dress correctly and act politely. It's also courteous to ask for permission before taking images of someone, especially in personal or private circumstances.

By being aware of and respecting the local traditions and etiquette, you may connect with the local culture more successfully and generate a favourable impression. Embrace the chance to learn from and respect the traditions of Barcelona and Madrid, and enjoy your stay in these dynamic cities.

CONCLUSION

In conclusion, Barcelona and Madrid provide many experiences, rich histories, dynamic cultures, and outstanding sights that make them must-visit tourist destinations. Whether you prefer to explore the intriguing alleyways of Barcelona or immerse yourself in the cosmopolitan appeal of Madrid, both cities have something distinctive to offer.

In Barcelona, you may bask in the splendour of its magnificent beaches, explore famous architectural wonders like the Sagrada Familia and Park Güell, and unearth hidden jewels in its off-the-beaten-path spots. The city's eccentric museums and art galleries will capture art fans. At the same time, its culinary scene will thrill food lovers with its distinct cuisines and local markets.

On the other side, Madrid charms with its grandeur and cultural importance. Marvel at Prado Museum treasures, tour the old Royal Palace and rest in the lovely Retiro Park. The bright Puerta del Sol, Plaza Mayor, and Gran Via display the city's energetic atmosphere and architectural delights. Take advantage of the lovely Mercado de San Miguel, a feast for the senses.

Both towns offer a plethora of hidden gems and lesser-known attractions, enabling you to explore the local life beyond the main tourist destinations. The diverse eating experiences, from classic tapas to contemporary gourmet delights, will tickle your taste buds, and the local markets will immerse you in the dynamic culinary scene.

In addition to its renowned sites, Barcelona and Madrid offer a choice of cultural activities, including flamenco shows and live music performances that exhibit the lyrical rhythms and passionate emotions of Spanish culture. Immerse yourself in the local customs and festivals, where you may see the vivid festivities and immerse yourself in a happy environment.

To guarantee a successful and pleasurable vacation, it's vital to consider practical factors such as communication and internet access, money problems, health and safety precautions, and local traditions and etiquette. Being aware and respectful of the local culture may improve your travel experience and develop significant relationships with the people.

Barcelona and Madrid are not merely cities to visit; they are destinations to be experienced, with their distinctive combination of history, art, culture, food, and friendly hospitality. Whether you're a history buff, an art enthusiast, a culinary lover, or just want to immerse yourself in the lively Spanish way of life, these towns provide an extraordinary voyage of discovery.

So pack your luggage, start on a spectacular vacation, and let the charm of Barcelona and Madrid emerge before you. Let the gorgeous architecture, delectable food, passionate flamenco, and loving welcome of Spanish culture have a lasting effect on your heart and mind. Barcelona and Madrid await, eager to capture and inspire you with their timeless beauty and dynamic vitality.

Printed in Great Britain
by Amazon

24413362R00129